The parish church of St Margaret's, Dunham Massey, Altrincham where I became a member of Christ, as a baby in Holy Baptism.

Faith and Works
An Experience of God in Ministry

Faith and Works
An Experience of God in Ministry

John Neville Greaves

ATHENA PRESS
LONDON

Faith and Works
An Experience of God in Ministry
Copyright © John Neville Greaves 2007

All Rights Reserved

No part of this book may be reproduced in any form
by photocopying or by any electronic or mechanical means,
including information storage or retrieval systems,
without permission in writing from both the copyright
owner and the publisher of this book.

ISBN 10-digit: 1 84401 998 5
ISBN 13-digit: 978 1 84401 998 4

First Published 2007 by
ATHENA PRESS
Queen's House, 2 Holly Road
Twickenham TW1 4EG
United Kingdom

Printed for Athena Press

To Joy
Sine qua parum

Timperley Methodist church.
Through the ministry of which I came to faith in 1954.
Photograph by Valerie Laws.

Contents

Introduction	11
1. Salford, 1961–1963	13
2. Wythenshawe, Manchester, 1963–1973	34
3. Sadberge, County Durham, 1973–1978	76
4. Durham City, 1978–1994	89
5. Post-retirement Postlude	132

Introduction

> The only argument for Christianity that proves anything is that it works.[1]

For nearly two hundred years now the Christian Church has experienced a true shaking of its foundations, as new developments in science and philology have caused a profound reassessment of its beliefs. The consequent rise of a secular mindset among those who inform the thinking of the general public, most radically in Europe but increasingly worldwide, has led to the marginalisation of the Church and its authority. The Church's ministers and parish priests have suffered some confusion and loss of nerve. Does God still exist in any way recognisable to the 2,000-year-old tradition, or must His status in the twenty-first century be simply that of an emotionally useful fiction or a God in a deistically Olympian detachment from his creation?

This is an account of one man's experience of serving God as a priest in the Church over a small portion of that time and in a tiny part of the Lord's vineyard. It recounts how, through several varied posts, his many weaknesses and inadequacies were overridden by God, and how the power of the Holy Spirit came into the lives of many. It is not an autobiography in the usual sense, but a chronological record of a life offered, after several years of scorn and rejection of the gospel, as a channel and an agent of an almighty God: a God who works through a Church which is both human and divine, both part of time and transcending material duration. It is a matter-of-fact glorification of the eternal loving Father, faithful to His promises, who loved His creation so much that He sent His Son in human flesh to redeem

---

[1] Owen Chadwick, in his book on John Henry Newman, Oxford University Press, 1983.

it and transfigure it, to reconcile it to Himself, to overcome its own self-contradictions, by whose Holy Spirit of truth His people are empowered to change the world. It is a testament of hope and glory to His fellow human beings and co-ministers of God's joy.

1

Salford, 1961–1963

> O world invisible, we view thee,
> O world intangible, we touch thee,
> O world unknowable, we know thee,
> Inapprehensible, we clutch thee.[1]

The city of Salford was known in the 1960s as 'the classic slum'.[2] I went there as a curate in 1961, which was immediately after the demolition of its most notorious area, Hankinson Park, where the docu-novel *Love on the Dole* was based; but there were still, and would be for several years to come, many square miles of *Coronation Street*-type terraced houses. There was an almost constant grey-black fog at roof level, the streets and buildings permanently begrimed by the coal dust content of the atmosphere. A local saying had it that when the fog was particularly thick at street level (as it was during November and December of 1961, after which I suffered a severe attack of bronchitis), it was possible to cut out a piece of it and burn it on the fire; a sort of recycling, hellwise. It was almost literally true. I had worked not far up the road in Manchester for thirteen years and experienced 'darkness at noon' – all street and vehicle lights fully on and midnight conditions at midday.

The mortality rate in Salford in 1960–62 was the worst in all the boroughs and county boroughs in England and Wales at the time: 46% above the average. The main cause was bronchitis, the

---

[1] Francis Thompson, 'The Kingdom of God', *Poems of Today* Sidgewick and Jackson: London, 1919, p.130.
[2] A book of that title, taking Salford as its subject, was a textbook for sociologists in the 1960s.

death rate from which was twice the national figure. The percentage of schoolchildren leaving at fifteen years of age or younger was 91.8 in the wards of Salford East. The percentage in Glasgow Shettleston, as a comparison, was 91.2.[3] Salford had also that other characteristic of 'the classic slum' – a great sense of neighbourliness. If Annie's milk had not been taken in off the doorstep, or Bertha's curtains were still drawn at 9 a.m., Lizzie next door would soon be enquiring if all was well. There was ready help in all difficulties. Married daughters (with the grandchildren) lived just around the corner and visited daily, to and fro. There was a keen overall awareness of belonging, and of mutual support. They were people who maintained a resignation with hopefulness, and a robust sense of humour which belied the social miseries and financial constraints of their lives. Some of the homes had no furniture other than the odd empty wooden box; at least one in our parish had no front door (canvas sacking instead), and no curtains, no stair banisters and no carpets (all burnt on the fire as fuel), and only a Stygian light bulb of about 1.5 watts. But they were at home; they felt secure. Despite the conditions, Salford people were lovely to live among, to work for, and with.

When the place began to be demolished, and the inhabitants were moved out to a lovely new council estate at Walkden (or, in the vernacular, 'Wogdin'), all that social cohesion was lost; they had shining new state-of-the-art houses, or, for those who didn't want to leave the area, multi-storey flats. But something wholesome had been lost. In 2002, Simon Jenkins wrote of witnessing 'the destruction of working class communities and their replacement by the new Jerusalem of the urban proletariat'; of seeing 'bulldozers moving across Walworth in South London and across Moss Side in Manchester' in the early 1970s; of 'watching people in tears being bussed like... refugees away from friendship and families and from any hope of informal employment'.[4]

---

[3] Peter Townsend, *Poverty in the United Kingdom*, London, Allen Lane, 1979, pp.951–952.
[4] Simon Jenkins, *Remaking the Landscape: The Changing Face of Britain*, ed. Jennifer Jenkins, Profile Books, 2002. A few years later, I, with one or two other clergy, made representation to the Manchester Housing Department to make some effort,

St Ambrose's, Salford

I had been invited by the Reverend Charles Allan Shaw to work with him in this unprepossessing area. A Cambridge rowing blue, six foot four and a Lancashire man, he had been the chaplain of Malvern College for four or so years, and had then approached the bishop of Manchester for the most 'difficult' parish he had vacant at the time. St Ambrose's, Pendleton, on Salford's Liverpool Street in the district of Seedley, had been damaged by bombs during the war, and the vicarage had perished altogether. A faithful priest, Father 'Bobby' Dodds, had ministered there from 1947 to 1956, living in a terraced house while the rebuilding of the vicarage was being organised, but takers for the parish when he left were hard to find. Allan Shaw was inducted in 1958, and it wasn't long before he had amassed, with his insight into the minds of teenagers, a youth club of some three hundred street-

---

when they moved people out to the estates, to place former neighbours in some contiguity. To their credit, they did adopt this suggestion, and it made a difference.

corner lads and their girls.[5] Before they were allowed to enjoy the club activities on a Sunday evening, they had to attend a Gospel service, held after Evensong. This was a short service of hymns, prayers, and an address which was an introduction to the nature and relevance of the Christian faith.

In our discussions before I committed myself to becoming his assistant, he made it clear that, contrary to the customary arrangement, I was not to concern myself with the youth work (apart from confirmation classes), because that was the main thrust of his ministry. This suited me well because I had prayed, during my last term at college preceding ordination, that I would never be required to (a) have anything to do with youth, having no talent for it; or (b) have responsibility for a churchyard, for there was more than sufficient work to be done with the living without spending whole stretches of time on the dead. Events were to teach me that one does not bargain with God, or hedge around one's discipleship with conditions.

I was made deacon on 28 May 1961 at an ordination service which was putatively the first in history to be televised. I have several photographs of the event, taken by a parishioner from the TV screen, complete with the pattern of his sofa faithfully reflected on the back of the bishop's head. On starting work in the parish I was given a list of people to visit by Allan Shaw. I soon became able to spot the house I was looking for from quite a distance (there were forty-odd houses on each side of several of the streets) by the newly painted woodwork and window sills – obvious respectability. This prompted me to reflect on whether church membership was a form of assumed respectability and, further, did that exclude church people from being considered as 'real' working class? If so, those in enclosed academic or ecclesiastical circles who claimed from time to time that the Church of England was 'not touching the working classes' were, by that circular argument, quite right. It seemed to me, adopting my own rule-of-thumb classification, that there were three kinds of people

---

[5] It was featured in a two-page article in the News Chronicle in September 1960. The newspaper folded not many months later, but Allan insisted that the two events were not connected.

who could be called working class.[6] There was the 'aspiring' working class (later to be termed 'upwardly mobile'), working for better standards in everything for themselves and their children. There was the 'contented' working class who didn't aspire at all except to have a job and keep it, and who on the whole were a great element of stability and reliability in society. And then there were the feckless and largely inadequate, who struggled with life and relied upon others or the state to keep them afloat.[7] Category one was perhaps the largest, and category three by far the smallest.

Aside from these semantic quibbles, a more significant sense of unease was revived by my visiting, originating from the time in my mid-teens when I rejected the Church and its God. At the age of fourteen, after some years in the Sunday school and the Boys' Brigade of the Methodist chapel which my mother attended,[8] I decided that Christianity was only for women and children and the socially immature. It was thus a sensitive nerve which was touched when, in response to my knock on the door in visiting, the man of the house appeared, took one look at me, and said over his shoulder, 'Mabel, it's for you!' and promptly disappeared to the back of the house. About the third time this happened, I followed him in, saying, 'Hang on, it's for you, too.' The abashed reply on this occasion, and in all subsequent similar exchanges, was along the lines of 'Church is my wife's hobby – mine's the pools/greyhounds/horses,' etc. Geoffrey Studdert-Kennedy, the great army chaplain known as 'Woodbine Willie' to the troops in the trenches of the First World War, was troubled by this image of

---

[6] Sidestepping Marx's definition, that working class people were those who had to sell their labour to live.

[7] Society has changed immensely since those days, and such sociological divisions are more complicated. I have always thought, however, that 'civilised refinement' and 'yob culture' are not confined by class at all.

[8] She was an Anglican, but on moving to Timperley in 1935 she joined the Methodist Chapel, which, being in the centre of the village, was more the 'parish church' at that time, and also had a very good choir (she was a semi-professional singer). She was brought up a member of St Margaret's, Dunham, Altrincham, where her parish priest was Hewlett Johnson. He and his wife ran holiday camps in North Wales for young people, and was a great influence and highly thought of in the parish. He was later dean of Manchester and then of Canterbury, where he achieved notoriety as 'The Red Dean'. He died on my birthday in 1966, aged ninety-two..

the Church in the eyes of the soldiers, who associated the chaplain immediately with the Mothers' Union. He wrote a book on the subject, *The Warrior, the Woman and the Child*,[9] which even now makes interesting reading, and still speaks to an unresolved debate.

A memorable encounter took place within a fortnight of arriving in the parish. Allan Shaw took me to be introduced to the rural dean of Salford, Gwilym Morgan,[10] and this entailed a visit to his curate, who was upstairs in bed, incapacitated with an infection. We found that gentleman propped up by pillows and surrounded by books. Allan said, 'What are you doing here? You should be out there,' (pointing to a block of high-rise flats hard by the rectory), 'spreading the gospel!' The curate replied, 'Oh, those people don't want me in their homes, preaching something which is irrelevant to their lives.' I didn't say anything, as befitted the new kid on the block, but my immediate thought was that I had just committed my life to doing just that – in the belief that the gospel was just as relevant to them as it was to everyone. Over the next year or so I got to know that curate better, and found him a highly intelligent and charming man; but Don Cupitt was to go on to make a name for himself in his rejection of the traditional message and his quest for something more 'real' and relevant.

Allan sent me to Canon Lionel Hussey at Sacred Trinity, Salford,[11] for instruction in how to don Eucharistic vestments. St Ambrose's, though of a liberal Catholic tradition, was not able to afford vestments until the next incumbency. Hussey was well-known in convocation and on civic occasions for perceptive and witty speeches. On my first visit to a hospital I met him again. I was in a single ward at the top of a flight of stairs, helping a nurse, at her request, who was trying to raise the foot of a bed and place

---

[9] Geoffrey Studdert-Kennedy, The Warrior, the Woman and the Child, London, Hodder and Stoughton Ltd, 1928.
[10] Rector of St Philip and St Stephen, Salford, 1954–1971, and rural dean of Salford from 1957–1971.
[11] Sacred Trinity had seen some very notable priests in its time. Hussey was there from 1931–1962, and Canon Peter Green from 1901–1911, when he moved the short distance to St Philip's, staying there, despite offers of at least one bishopric, until 1951. Both names still resonate in Salford and Manchester.

supports under the legs. I held up the bed while she put them in place. At that moment Canon Hussey came up the stairs and didn't reply to my cheery 'Hello'. Later, on the ward, he asked me, in a proper Church of England voice, 'What were you doing with that nurse?' On hearing my explanation, he replied, 'A clergyman does not do that kind of thing.' Oh dear, I thought. Improper behaviour and a lack of a Church of England voice – perhaps I wasn't going to make the grade at all.

The terraced house the parish had bought for us,[12] in which we lived for the two and a half years we were there, was just over the border into the next parish. Allan had told us it was in Haven Street, on sale by Paradise Estates, in a parish whose incumbent was a Mr Moon, which sounded quite heavenly. This afforded us a front garden, three feet long and as wide as the frontage of the house, though it still had the traditional backyard (and a dysfunctional outside toilet), letting on to a 'back entry' – a passage running parallel with the street and common to the backyards of the houses in the next street. Just before I set off for my pre-ordination retreat I popped in there to see if all was well for my wife Joy and our little daughter to move in. I noticed that the back door was open. A break-in, I thought, with perception worthy of Sherlock Holmes himself, and set off to find the nearest policeman, who happened to be on point duty a hundred yards away at the Langworthy Road/Liverpool Street crossroads. Having seen the rush hour safely through, he came to make notes of my statement, and when we looked in the cellar we saw that the gas and electricity meters had been broken into, and the contents stolen. He then asked, with true constabulary suspicion, what I was doing around at that time of day. As soon as I had explained he became trust and confidentiality itself, saying it all bore the hallmarks of the previous occupant, who had been released from Strangeways a day or so before. It was an introduction to our new house which was designed to win us from the comfort of the leafy Cheshire suburbs we had been used to (though our accommodation for the last year of college life had been not dissimilar – a terraced house in Tranmere, Birkenhead, without electricity and with an intransigent landlady).

The general condition of the house was appalling. The last

---

[12] For £600.

owner had used the front room as a chicken pen, and it was six or nine inches deep in soil, covered with droppings, though the parish ladies had cleaned out and swept it into numerous bags which lay in the backyard. One of the key people in the parish was Amy Stansfield, a genuine leader, an indefatigable worker and a dead ringer for Violet Carson, who played Ena Sharples in the early days of *Coronation Street*. Violet Carson had been, in former times, a pianist for silent films at the Langworthy Cinema, on Langworthy Road in the parish.

We shared our house with mice and cockroaches, and regular and frequent burst pipes. One morning the living room carpet greeted us from beneath an inch of water, the electric fittings smoked unhealthily, and the roofs leaked, front and back – the latter flooding the ceiling over our daughter's cot and filling the light bulb, which exploded when switched on. When the pipes were being repaired, the dust permeated everywhere, especially when a burst pipe under the concrete floor in the kitchen caused the wholesale removal of the floor and part of the wall. I had to sleep downstairs in front of the fire the whole night on one occasion, keeping our newborn son warm because he was suffering some sort of chest infection. The walls were continually damp, and the windows and doors were so ill fitting that draughts and dirt flew in all over the place. Silver fish (which I had never heard of before, though Joy had, in her days as a district midwife and health visitor) scuttled about cheerfully, and a further enlargement of my understanding of natural history came with the ritual dances of snails and slugs on the living room carpet each night. Their silver trails led from the battered skirting boards to the middle of the room, where a large area of slime seemed to tell of conjugal, or at least terpsichorean, bliss. That was soon cured (unlike most of the other problems): I placed salt round each hole until I found their entrance and then blocked up all the holes.

Our daughter Jillian went out to play in sparkling cleanliness each day only to return every few minutes for something to drink, covered in grime – her face, her hands, her clothes. At first, Joy would wash and change her each time, but it wasn't long before she gave up that road to a nervous breakdown, and conformed to local custom. It made us realise that slum conditions were prior to 'slum dwellers', and not the other way round. Towards the end of our stay the carrycot wheels and Jillian's dolls' pram containing her two favourite dolls were stolen, as was the football of our little son Jonathan. But everyone suffered that kind of offence. Joy did have occasional attacks of catatonia when it all got on top of her, explaining later that conditions had been far better on the mission field in Nigeria, lizards and scorpions notwithstanding.

The irony is that after I had accepted the vicar's offer of a curacy at St Ambrose's,[13] just before ordination, I had been given an invitation to consider going instead to Prestwich Parish Church, Manchester. That was a considerably well-heeled parish with a prestigious rectorial appointment,[14] and the temptation was vivid. However, I had given my word to the first man, and Joy agreed that to regard our own comfort and convenience as part of a genuine 'call' from God seemed to be special pleading or simply worldly temptation. She had committed herself to God at the age of seven to qualify as a nursing missionary, ready to go anywhere when the time came, and the promise held good.[15] Dr Billy Greer, bishop of Manchester, used to say wistfully in his Dublin brogue that when he enquired of his ordinands where they were going to serve their title (first curacy), they mostly replied that they were 'leaving that to the Holy Spirit'. It was surprising, he told me, how often the Holy Spirit led them to Guildford diocese.

Not long into our time in the parish, Matthew Deas, the rector of the mother church of the parishes of Pendleton, conceived the idea that the local clergy should go once a week into the new secondary modern school, Clarendon, to teach the *Book of*

---

[13] The system was that a vicar wanting a curate would make enquiry of a theological college principal, setting out the sort of person that the job would need. It was not, in those days, considered the done thing to try to influence such invitations. It is not surprising either, that these days the spouse and children involved have a greater say, the old military/monastic ethos having been thoroughly eclipsed.

[14] The Rector had been previously the predecessor of Canon Eric Saxon, my mentor, at St Ann's Manchester.

[15] In case this sounds too twee on our part, I ought to admit that neither of us knew at that time what Salford held in store for us, in terms of living conditions.

Common Prayer in the RE period. The auguries were not good. The father of a pupil at the next school geographically, on the docks, had recently threatened a teacher with a knife for punishing his son. This engagement was my first regular spell of teaching in schools, though we had done some teaching practice at theological college. I was given the top class, the sixteen-year-olds, purely because I was lost in the rush to 'bag' the youngest ones. To my surprise, after the first two or three weeks of desk-lid banging, missile projection, and the funny comments in carefully disguised voices while my back was turned, some sort of order began to emerge. By the end of the first year, when the lads (the girls were in a separate school across the playing field) came to leave, some of them were shedding tears when we said our farewells. This pattern was to be repeated in the following year, when again I had the sixteen-year-olds. By that time the number of clergy had dropped to two: myself and Allan Shaw who was doing great things with the same lads as last year, having moved up with them. He was replaced in due course by his successor at St Ambrose's, Richard Palmer, who in his own inimitable way (he taught them yoga in the gym) also made an impact. The problems for the other brethren was that they didn't cope well with the lads, and asked to be transferred to the girls' classes, not realising that they were in for far more difficult problems. They lasted an even shorter time there. I missed the experience when I left Salford, greatly to my surprise: it went a long way towards opening up an interest and confidence in youth work. My forays into teaching in schools were only intermittent thereafter.

The founder of the famous group of holiday camps, Billy Butlin, was not as well-known as he ought to have been as a great benefactor of charities and needy causes. One of these, in his eyes, was that of curates in inner-city parishes who, more than most of their coevals, needed a sunshine break, and if they had small children, could not afford one. He offered a free holiday at one of his camps, and we chose Pwllheli in North Wales, simply because it was the nearest and therefore involved the cheapest rail fare. Despite our minimum expectations (Lord forgive us!) and the fact that we would be living in 'terraced chalets', and of course the regimentation of *reveille* and mealtimes, we had a very restful and enjoyable time. At one of the evening theatre entertainments I found myself sitting behind Charles Davidson, who was by then reporting the entertainment scene for the *Daily Express* (if my memory serves). The importance of this man in my spiritual history ought at this stage to be expounded, and although this is not an autobiography as such, I need to fill in some background.

My mother was a distant relative of the English composer and organist Herbert Howells, and the house was always full of music. After my childhood it took years for me to get interested again in 'Messiah', 'Elijah', 'Creation' and the songs of Haydn Wood, Michael Head, Elgar, Cecille Chaminade and the like. My father was passionately fond of brass and military bands and their repertoire of 'Pique Dame', 'Ruy Blas', 'Poet and Peasant', 'The Bronze Horse', 'Light Cavalry' and all their stablemates. I graduated early via the wartime 'Victory' motif of Beethoven's Fifth Symphony to his other symphonies, and via Schubert, Schumann, Brahms, Dvorak to the heavier side of things – Bruckner, Mahler, Schoenberg and into the twentieth century. Both my sisters sang, and the elder, Pauline, was also a competent pianist and accompanist. However, the younger, Christine, remarked at the age of sixteen or so, 'I don't like this twelve-stone music (a reference to Schoenberg); it is too heavy for me,' and took her musical education no further.[16] During my years of unbelief and searching for the basic sense in the world, music was the only thing that kept me going. I reasoned that there must be intelligence beyond all this life and death and evolution and extinction if we can sense it through such beautiful creations, such combinations of powerful emotion and intellectual organisation. Beethoven said that 'Music is philosophy in sound', and that was my sole take on reality in those years. I divided my leisure hours between writing my own music and fulfilling my resolution, on leaving Army National Service, to read through at least one text of all the great philosophers as a grossly belated start to serious education. Many years later I discovered that Siegfried Sassoon had expressed my position far better than I, when he wrote,

---

[16] Though her four children, in the 1970s, formed a group, singing and recording their own compositions.

> When selfhood can discover no comfort for its cares,
> Whither may I turn to you whose strength my spirit shares?
> Where may I find but in you, Beethoven, Bach, Mozart[...][17]
>
> The subsistence of my dreams took fire. Timeless, eternally true,
> You built cathedrals in my heart
> And for my pinnacled desire you were the ardour and the bright
> Procession of my thoughts towards prayer.[18]

Even more profoundly, David Gascoyne expressed it thus:

> Supernal voices flood the ear of clay
> And transpierce the dense skull: Reveal
> The immaterial world concealed
> By mortal deafness and the screen of sense,
>
> World of transparency and last release
> And world within the world. Beyond our speech
> To tell the equinoxes of the infinite
> The spirit ranges in its rare utmost flight.[19]

My father, after the war, became a sports coach to our Boys' Brigade company, steering us through youth competitions and getting admirable results, season by season, from the soccer team in the local youth league. He even started attending church, feeling that it would be a bad example to the lads if he didn't, though Pauline told me years later that he didn't believe in anything spiritual, having been since his teens a convinced down-to-earth practical Sheffield socialist (the only member of the extended family of grandfathers and uncles who was not a convinced Tory). One day, in 1953, the Methodist Minister, John Stacey, came to see my parents in the course of visiting his flock, and was surprised to find that there was a son in the family. I was sitting reading an Aldous Huxley novel,

---

[17] From Siegfried Sassoon's 'Strangeness of Heart'.
[18] From Siegfried Sassoon's 'Dead Musicians'.
[19] From 'Mozart: Sursum Corda'.

and he asked me why he hadn't seen me before. I told him that it was quite simple – I didn't believe. 'I've just started a study group at the manse for young adults – would you like to join us?' he said. My reply was that I would spoil it for everyone else, with my sour scepticism. 'Come along all the same,' he replied. 'We might learn from each other.' Well, at this stage I've nothing to lose, I thought. I may as well go along. And so I did. The meetings proceeded as turbulently as I had warned but most of the group were familiar to me from the village and we were good friends. My membership did not last long. After leaving the army I had been with Sale Harriers as a middle-distance runner (and on one occasion at the Cheshire Championships, as a discus thrower), and just before Christmas 1953 I began to feel below par in the cross-country races. A visit to the doctor diagnosed bilateral pulmonary tuberculosis. I was packed off to the Cheshire Joint Sanatorium (Shropshire/Staffordshire) at Market Drayton, where the doctor explained that as my condition was too serious for surgery, and the new drugs were not yet proven in effectiveness, I ought to be reconciled to whatever happened. I wandered down the corridor to complete bed rest for some months. The Methodist group took it in turns to write me a report of each meeting's discussion, and several of them visited me. John Stacey sent me suitable reading matter, notably C S Lewis's *Mere Christianity*[20] and *Miracles*. After about eight months I became perambulant about the hospital and was elected chairman of the Patients' Committee – the youngest ever, apparently – representing the patients on meetings with the staff, helping the library visitors, doing jobs in the main office block, and being the editor of the sanatorium magazine.

Relationships with the other patients were excellent, as was fitting, but there was one exception. Charles ('Dave') Davidson, a man of my own height and build and stubbornness, who had been the Northern Area Amateur Ballroom Champion (if my recollection is accurate), decided he didn't like me and whenever we met it must have been clear to onlookers that we were not each other's favourite person. If memory serves correctly, the mutual disrespect dated back to a heated discussion of his

---

[20] Published eighteen months before.

statement that Charlie Chaplin was a greater composer than Beethoven, because the theme from the film *Limelight* was selling more records than anything by Beethoven. On one occasion, when nearly all the other patients were at a concert in the sanatorium theatre, he challenged me to a game of chess. The atmosphere was charged with electric hostility, far more so than in any of the boxing matches I had been involved in during my army days. After something like an hour and a half I was able to say 'Checkmate' and walk out without a further word, bursting with an awful pride and leaving behind me an atmosphere heaving with vitriol. Later, we were both in a row of chalets away from the main wards – the last 'station' on the journey towards release – I at the far end, he nearest the main building. His had been the 'duty morning', making early tea for those who couldn't function without it, and as I passed on my way to the administration block he said, 'Will you take this teapot back for me?' The day before, I had been reading one of the C S Lewis's books lent to me by John Stacey and had come to the conclusion that it seemed as though 'Love' was the key – not intellectual rigour and conviction, but loving the Other as oneself in humility and surrender.[21] I had said to God, 'If you exist and are listening, I will try to live by this love tomorrow, for one day. If it is true, make it clear. If nothing happens, I'll go on searching.' I had been put to the test immediately. My instinctive reaction to Dave's request was one of immediate hostility. But I reminded myself of the previous day's promise. 'Yes, certainly,' I replied, picking up the teapot and setting off up the short path to the administration block. On that cold, damp, dark day of 12 September 1954 at 8.50 a.m., I experienced a sudden enlightenment and conviction that 'It's all true!' and the sky seemed to brighten beautifully. I walked vigorously through the doors, and someone standing inside exclaimed, 'What's happened to you?' I don't remember what I said, but I knew for certain that there was a God, that Jesus was right all along, and that no matter what life was to bring, I was His, completely.

---

[21] See The Cloud of Unknowing: 'Of God himself can no man think [...] by love he can be taught and held, but by thinking, never.'

One of the jobs of the Patients' Committee chairman was to take the service in the sanatorium chapel on a Sunday evening (the Sunday morning service was taken by an ordained minister of one of the local denominations). These services were always well attended, mainly because they were the only occasion when men and women patients could meet unsupervised by staff. I had never attended before, naturally, but now it fell to me to prepare and lead a service. Well, you never know, I thought, the experience might come in handy sometime.[22]

I was a bit put off on the first occasion by the books of 'messages' used by my predecessors as a resource in place of a sermon. They dated from the early 1940s and were full of unreconstructed moral uplift for use during bombing raids, gas attacks and invasion by paratroopers. I felt that although the lads and lasses may not notice all the anachronisms and anomalies, having, as they did, eyes only for each other, those addresses would not do. So I took to using C S Lewis's *Mere Christianity*, which was also written under wartime conditions, but it didn't show, presenting instead the eternal truths in a way which had opened me up to new possibilities. The response was surprising: everyone paid attention and several enquired afterwards what I was reading from.

From 12 September 1954 the world felt and looked fresh and new and hopeful. I didn't know the term at that time, but it really seemed like being born again. I did not have a sense of sin – confessed or forgiven. That came later, very strongly, during the Prayer of Humble Access at my first communion service in the Methodist church after getting home. The serious stuff was still to come. At the time the whole experience was of childlike joy and rebirth. To get back to Pwllheli, 1962: I found myself sitting

---

[22] Though I remember distinctly that I had made it clear to God on 12 September that (a) my life was at His disposal, to use as He would, but that (b) I would never be a parson. I struggled to decide, over the next two and a half years, on the denomination to which I should commit myself (attending services of a very wide variety of congregations), and for my exact calling. The outcome was that I was confirmed (with Joy) in Manchester Cathedral on 9 December 1957, accepted for ordination five weeks later, cancelled the place I had been offered at Chester College to train as a teacher (the last attempt to avoid 'becoming a parson'), and went to St Aidan's Theological College, Birkenhead in October 1958.

behind the aforementioned Charles ('Dave') Davidson, and astonished and pleased to be able to round off our clashings with a happy ending. It was not to be. Although I told him who I was, and what had happened, and expressed a warm recollection of the enormously important part he had unwittingly played in my life, he was cold and hostile. I could hardly have expected him to be otherwise. I was glad to have met him again, though.

Salford had other learning curves for me to negotiate. Callous violence was something neither of us was used to, though we had both previously worked late hours in Manchester and seen drunken brawls and policemen being overwhelmed by the unprincipled. Early in my time in the parish, I was walking home after an afternoon's visiting when I noticed in a side street a huge crowd of youngsters, screaming and shouting. I made my way through them all to the middle, thinking to break it up if it was a fight. But when I got there, it was not two boys but two girls, screeching and scratching, pulling hair and kicking. I had never before seen girls fighting, and it quite unnerved me. I withdrew, the crowd closing behind me like water behind the passage of a ship, and made my way to church to say Evensong with the vicar. I told him of the incident, and he rebuked me, saying 'You ought to have broken it up – we do stand for something, you know.' He was quite right, of course.[23]

In January 1962, we had a parish visit from some Lincoln Theological College students, preparing for ordination. When, in 1958, I had been offered a choice of three colleges, I chose St Aidan's, Birkenhead, because, as I was newly married, it was the nearest of the three; one of the others was Lincoln. Meeting students from there (Allan and I returned the visit a month or so later), was a good experience for me, especially as they 'sat in' (unknowingly) on my very first confirmation class. Lincoln

---

[23] Forty years later houses in the parish were selling for £1600, or 'two for the price of one', though it was said that 'down the pub' it was possible to buy one for £700 (at a time when the average house price in England was £75,000). About that time, a BBC film unit was sent to the parish for a study in the series *Poverty in Britain*, but the team was mugged and had to leave and think of somewhere safer to make their film. 'Like Beirut or Bosnia?' suggested the news commentator.

would have provided us with married quarters, but St Aidan's was special, and produced a distinctive kind of priest. This was due, I think, to two things. One was its foundation in 1847 with the specific intention of training men who were not graduates of Oxford or Cambridge, for ministry in the North of England, as St Aidan had been the 'Apostle of the North'; and the other was the quality of leadership which set the tradition of the college, represented at the time by Canon 'Gerald' Scott.[24] He had set a magisterial standard of scholarship and discipline for the college during his nine-year tenure, and he was succeeded by his deputy Michael Hennell.[25] Both convinced Evangelicals, they had nevertheless maintained a policy of having a hefty proportion of students from liberal and Anglo-Catholic backgrounds, and the chapel had been reordered on modern liturgical principles, with a free-standing altar and Laudian drape, and two stone ambos. This meant that, learning together, we became acquainted with, and appreciative of, in charity, the different strands of churchmanship in the Church of England. Michael was a supreme example of Christian humility, pastoral care and wisdom. One example of his Catholic breadth was to send six of us in our final year to stay a few days in Halton, a large council estate in Leeds, where Canon Ernest Southcott, a man of Canadian exuberance, was leading an interesting exploration of the parish as a revolutionary community. His book on the work he was doing there, *The Parish Comes Alive*,[26] described how he came to realise that the parish was the pattern of a fully human community, the pattern of all true community, centred as it was on Christ the Creator God. His book still makes helpful reading as a theological tract and inspiration for ministry, though its detailed application would be

---

[24] William Morris Fitzgerald Scott, principal from 1950 until his untimely death in 1959. I was the last student he admitted, in October 1958. I met him on my introductory visit to the college, when he welcomed me with a strong handshake, saying simply, 'Scott – Principal'. I was immediately taken by that economical and forthright greeting.

[25] Michael Murray Hennell (1918–1996): St Aidan's College 1951–63; principal, Ridley Hall, Cambridge 1963–1970; canon residentiary of Manchester Cathedral, 1970–84; biographer of Henry Venn, one of the earliest Anglican Evangelicals and founder of the 'Clapham Sect'.

[26] Mowbrays, 1956.

impossibly daunting in these days of multiple responsibilities and the increasing secularisation of our culture. It represented the high point of the Anglo-Catholic Anglican establishment, and its presuppositions are perhaps not as secure now. 'Ernie' Southcott wrote to me shortly after the visit to offer me a curacy, but I was committed to St Ambrose's. By the time of my second curacy he had been whisked off to be the provost of Southwark Cathedral, South London.

Allan Shaw departed from the parish in September 1962, having been 'headhunted' to be the chaplain and assistant to Leonard Wilson, the bishop of Birmingham.[27] The rural dean informed me that the bishop of Manchester wanted me to be the priest in charge during the interregnum, so I took over the reins with far more quietness of mind than my three months as a priest qualified me for. The first thing that happened was that the great youth club, that monument to an extraordinary period of ministry which had produced altar boys and crucifers with sideburns and winkle-pickers – to the delight of the daughters of the bishops of Manchester and Middleton – evaporated, almost overnight. Some of the lads remained, however, and a youth club consisting of members of the uniformed organisations and the choirgirls formed the nucleus of a more conventional kind of youth work. I still met the previous lads from time to time on street corners, but clearly the charisma of Allan Shaw's leadership had not passed to me. On the other hand, there emerged an unsuspected and unlooked-for talent for 'being good with young people,' to quote a reported remark of one youngster to those of Peel Hall when they visited my new parish after I left. (In completion of the equation, I was also to inherit large churchyard responsibilities in my third and fourth parishes, with equally surprising equanimity: truly the Lord does not call those who are fit, but fits those whom he calls.)

---

[27] 1953–1969. Formerly bishop of Singapore (1941–1948) and of a Japanese prisoner of war camp (1943), and dean of Manchester (1948–1953). Charles Allan Shaw (1927–1989) was subsequently dean of Bulawayo, (1967–75), archdeacon of Bulawayo, (1969–75), canon residentiary of Hereford, (1975–82), dean of Ely (1982–83), and P-in-C of Alcester, Warwickshire from 1984 to his sudden death in 1989.

Early in 1963 a new vicar was appointed to St Ambrose's. Richard Warwick Palmer,[28] another Cambridge man, an old boy of King's School, Wimbledon, had just completed a curacy in Hull. He too was not married, but there the resemblances ended. Allan Shaw had taught me the professionalisms of the job – wise counsel on what to avoid doing or saying, potential pitfalls for the novice, checking on a Saturday morning that the text of what I was going to preach on the following day was in accordance with gospel truth and sound tradition (he once sent me back to write a sermon on John the Baptist, Advent 4, on 23 December when the one I had written was on Christmas), acquainting me with the law of the land as it impinged on the Church (which set me in good stead for those laws affecting marriage, for which later I became a surrogate), and generally imparting to me the principles of 'best practice' in the conduct of services and my own pastoral and administrative work. Richard, on the other hand, was artistic, creative, filled with such a trust in God that he was heedless of the effect his openness, honesty and fervour would have on people. Joy (especially) and I both learned much from his approach to ministry, without my taking my feet off the bottom, so to speak. He particularly endeared himself to her by addressing immediately the parlous state of the curacy house.

In 1963 I entered the final year of formal post-ordination training, and in our third year we were allowed to choose a subject of our own particular interest. I chose Metaphysics, requesting Professor Dorothy Emmett of Manchester University as tutor. A rather dry-sounding subject, but it had roots in my past. During my National Service in the army I had come across a Pelican book *Plato and his Dialogues*, and made a resolution that after demobilisation I would set myself to read at least one work by every prominent philosopher from Heraclitus to date, as

---

[28] Later to become Mapplebeckpalmer when he married Lindzi Mapplebeck on 29 April 1973, at a ceremony in the church which, by any account, must rank as unique. Richard wrote it himself, incorporating prayers and declarations from many sources, and it was administered by two bishops (Manchester and Middleton), an Eastern Orthodox cantor, a rabbi, an Anglican priest, and the minister of the local Congregational church. The couple were married under a Jewish 'Orthodox Home' canopy.

mentioned previously.[29] By the time Richard came, I had got to Hegel and one of his English followers, F H Bradley; Richard Palmer's arrival was a challenge to me, by his method of 'simply following faith'. It clashed with my need for a 'metaphysic', a framework within which to interpret theology – pastoral, ethical and theoretical – in a coherent way.

Richard said at the outset that I had more experience of running a parish than he had, and was willing to be in learning mode while we were together, particularly as he needed, as he put it, 'reining in' a bit at times. He was to be there for a long stretch[30] because he was not easy to place anywhere else. We left the parish later that year with fond memories echoing in our minds and hearts; memories of Richard, of Allan Shaw's part in my professional formation, and of the hard but beneficial experience of having lived in the last days of the old 'Industrial Revolution' lifestyle and environment of a notable Northern city. I feel proud to have served, in a small way, the people of Salford for that time, especially when one now sees the enormous strides the city has made in rebuilding itself, and developing the docks area so beautifully. The last house visit I paid in Salford was to a young couple who wanted to make arrangements for a baptism. They lived overlooking the River Irwell and Manchester Cathedral – not in our parish, but they had been married at St Ambrose's three or four years earlier. The lad was a Mancunian, the girl from Salford, and he was quick to point out the difference between the two types: he was quick-witted and crafty, married to someone who was 'thick' – his word, not responded to by his wife. Salford people (great generalisation coming) were more like country folk: homely, gentle and immediately likeable. Manchester folk (another generalisation) were 'city': streetwise, a step ahead at all times, clever and vigorous; all the virtues, in fact, which made

---

[29] This was not only as a search for the meaning of life, but as a basis for getting an education, having left school at fourteen.

[30] 1963–1977. He went to be priest in charge of Ambrosden, etc, in the Oxford diocese, where he remained from 1977 to 1988, before going to the USA. His personality and methods were such that he split people into two camps – those who supported him wholeheartedly in goodwill, and those who could not understand him at all.

Manchester the world's first example of industrial enterprise and organisation and the first exponents of Adam Smith's free market capitalism. We were to experience the differences within a few days of moving to Manchester.

2

Wythenshawe, Manchester, 1963–1973

> Not by power, not by might, but by my Spirit, says the Lord Almighty.[1]

> This all-surpassing power is from God and not from us.[2]

The arrival of a new vicar at St Ambrose's set in motion the arrangements for my being sent to another parish. Richard Warwick Palmer was three years younger than I, this was his first living, and as I had been priest in charge of the parish for some months he decided to 'let himself in' slowly. He was full of zest for the job and brimming with creative ideas, as well as considerable boyish charm and a very firm faith. Faced with problems, he always said 'Jahweh Jireh' – 'the Lord will provide' (Genesis 22:8) – and of course He always did.

The Bishop of Manchester asked me on 22 May 1963 to go and see him to discuss the future. He would like me to go, he said, to St Luke's Benchill, Wythenshawe, in response to a request from the vicar there for someone who would take charge of the Peel Hall area of the parish, and take it to independence. St Luke's had a population of over 31,000 (which meant eight or nine weddings each Saturday in the high season, plus many funerals), and it seemed a good idea to take out of it an area which divided off fairly cleanly and took a third of those people with it. 'I want you to consider it, Greaves,' said the bishop, 'and unless you have a good reason not to, you are to go there.' There was nothing unusual, or objectionable, in such an address in those days. Our

---

[1] Zechariah 4:6
[2] 2 Corinthians 4:7

training for the ministry was semi-monastic in ethos, and we were men under orders as well as in orders. In 1958, when I entered theological college, bishops were still empowered to veto a student's desire to get married before his ordination, and to check that the intended woman was suitable.

Unfortunately, he gave the vicar of Benchill an inflated report of my capabilities: the first two years there were punctuated by attempts by the incumbent to discredit my character and motives with the people of the new area, a policy which divided them immediately into two camps. But there was great exhilaration in the adventure of starting off a new parish. We inherited a Sunday School hall, built by the previous vicar of St Luke's, Canon Stanley Mitchell – a pleasant brick-built affair, with a recessed porch, two side rooms and a fair-sized rear meeting room, in addition to the main hall with a dais at the far end. This building served as a dual-purpose parish hall and place of worship until we had arrived at the stage where we could contemplate a purpose-built church.

Wythenshawe ('Willow Copse') is a V-shaped invasion by Manchester into Cheshire, bounded by the River Mersey in the north and Gatley Brook and Fairywell Brook on the east and west, comprising the ancient parish of Northenden.[3] The area had been bought by Manchester Corporation in 1926 for development as a garden city, and comprised 2,569 acres, augmented in 1936 by the purchase of a further 1,307 acres. In addition, the whole area of the Manchester Airport was absorbed in the county boundary adjustments of 1974.

The creation of a garden city, on the lines of Letchworth (1903) and Welwyn (1920) was a bold and visionary venture on the part of Manchester's civic leaders. The survivors of the trenches of the First World War returned home to houses that were dilapidated and unsanitary in the city's decaying slums.[4] As

---

[3] It was mostly the area of Northen Etchells – 'additional land extension to the parish of Northen(den)'. It comprised the areas of Sharston, Benchill, Lawton Moor, Crossacres, Woodhouse Park, and Peel Hall, with Newall Green, Baguley, Royal Oak, and part of Brooklands.

[4] Slum clearance in Manchester had begun in 1841. In 1864, 15,000 so-called 'cave dwellers' lived in Manchester cellars.

St Richard of Chichester, Wythenshawe, Manchester.

late as 1945, a third of Manchester's housing stock (68,000 dwellings) was unfit for human habitation. By 1937, many of the slum sufferers had been rehoused in Wythenshawe, a process which received renewed impetus after the Second World War.

The only village of note in the developing area was Northenden itself, on the 'Northen' boundary, the River Mersey, of the Saxon Kingdom of Mercia. To achieve its lebensraum, Manchester had a great struggle to wrest the land from the councils of Cheshire and Bucklow, but its incorporation was achieved by 1931, and by 1936 was complete. The diocese of Chester ceded the whole to the Manchester diocese in 1933. In terms of the improvement of social conditions it was indeed a praiseworthy conception, and overall a successful one, and this has to be borne in mind wherever the problems and pains are discussed.

The need was soon felt for employment opportunities, good transport facilities, for shops and recreation areas and for new churches,[1] as well as a proper focus for community life. This last emerged in the late 1960s with the development of the Civic Centre (happily, in our parish), and it included the imaginative venture of an 'outpost' of the Manchester Library Theatre Company, which staged many productions of the highest order.

Wythenshawe grew to become the largest municipal housing estate in the western hemisphere,[2] but the policy of breaking up one hundred-year-old communities in the city and placing them eight or nine miles away among strangers did not make for social cohesion. As early as the mid-1930s is was reported that vandalism and hooliganism were growing problems, and that empty houses were having to be demolished because of such activities.

---

[1] Half the bishop of Manchester's budget for new church building in 1937 was designated for Wythenshawe. Eventually, by 1974, there was a total of eight Anglican (and eight Roman Catholic) parishes in the garden city, plus about ten or eleven Free Church chapels.

[2] *The Guinness Book of Records* quotes Becontree Estate in Essex (Barking and Redbridge, built in 1929) as the largest. It gives the area as 1,600 acres on a site of 3,000 acres, 26,820 houses, and a population of 89,000. But the figures for Wythenshawe are 3,876 acres (excluding the airport area), 26,800 houses, and a population of 102,000.

In the 1950s the rector of Northenden attempted to fight it by appealing to parents to control their children. A city councillor remarked, after complaints from Gatley of cross-border marauding and other antisocial behaviour, that they were dismissible as 'the whinings of Cheshire snobs'. With such validation from authority it is hard to blame the youngsters entirely for thinking that such class warfare was a legitimate part of their leisure entertainment. In the mid-1970s, adventure playgrounds and public parks, facilities so very desirable in large communities, had to be closed because of wanton damage and other 'undesirable activities'. The fire brigade had the embarrassment of having their former fire station premises burnt down, and a praiseworthy attempt to encourage social events, the Wythenshawe Council, though successful for a few years, had to be discontinued in the face of rampant hooliganism. Many of the children, growing up in surroundings of clean air,[3] spacious roads with grass verges, houses with mod cons and gardens, seemed to react against the attempts to ameliorate their circumstances. There had grown up, by the early 1960s, a culture of contempt for respectability, which showed itself in knocking off the heads of flowers as they passed by, lobbing stones through windows whose curtains gave offence, and the verbal – sometimes physical – persecution of anyone who used words of more than two syllables.[4]

It soon became searingly obvious after our arrival that we were undergoing culture shock, too. Despite the contiguity of Salford and Manchester, and their Siamese twin relationship in the mind of most of the rest of England, the two had quite different characteristics. As against the smoky and gloomy atmosphere in Salford, Wythenshawe, in contrast, having been an area of open farmland with air fit for a TB sanatorium,[5] nearly 250 ft above sea level and in sight of Kinder Scout in the South Pennines, had a

---

[3] Though the Clean Air Acts of 1956 and 1968 (a process consolidated in 1993) had a dramatic effect on Salford and Central Manchester.

[4] Twenty years on, and counting, such hatred for 'elitism' has become more the norm, with bullying being the name of the game among children, and widespread unbridled self-expression and violence amongst adults generally.

[5] Baguley, built in 1905, used as a general hospital during the war, and later becoming the Wythenshawe hospital.

very positive atmosphere. But the people, as I have indicated earlier, were quite different. I remember the first youth dance I attended at St Luke's, and being rather alarmed at the sheer energy and menace of the event. When fights broke out they were vicious affairs, preceded by a gathering feeling of coldness and impending disaster, whereas fights during such events in Salford had no apparent build-up. Rather there would have been a sudden thud and a bent face, a temporary disruption of proceedings calmed by the motherly women of the congregation who were in attendance, and a peaceful resumption.

I soon got accustomed to the higher octane altitude however, and we started our own Peel Hall dances by opening the front doors one Friday evening and playing loud music (on a borrowed record player) into the surrounding darkness and the punters dribbled in in groups.

Eventually, over the following weeks and months we had 150 to 200 at a time. Our own dances were certainly Mancunian in texture, but I and the loyal team of church wardens (later augmented by some of the wives) and a group of our church-connected teenagers, learned how to stay becalmed and positive when mayhem broke out. The first thing when it did so was to ensure that the band or group continued playing; otherwise the battleground became the focus of everyone's attention, rather than the music. That rule was broken from our control only once, when one of the musicians had his face rearranged by a chair, and the whole group stopped playing and dived into the fray. The second rule was harder to learn; it was to foresee where the trouble was likely to come from and engage the suspect(s) in friendly conversation, to direct their thoughts elsewhere. One lad in particular had a very cool and businesslike attitude (quite unmalicious in a way), picking out from the crowd the lad he was going to 'sort out', and then wading through to get him. He was known as 'Rocky' (not his real name, but I promised never to divulge what it was), and he was indeed built like a rock, with unruly black hair and a permanent scowl. I learned that he came from a home where his father had habitually beaten him up, and it had become a way of life. He was, in fact, a nice lad beneath it all, and gave no more trouble once he had seen me as someone to talk to.

Another character who stood out was a very tall thin lad, about nineteen years old, going on forty-five in appearance. He had only one eye, a badly scarred face, wore battered jeans and motorbike boots, from one of which protruded a large knife. On his first visit he came right up to me and stood with his face about four inches from mine. We stood there for some seconds, he weighing the possibilities, and me relaxing into God, I hoped.

He said, 'What would you do if someone hit you now?'

I replied, from somewhere, 'It would depend on who it was.'

There was further glaring scrutiny of my face. Then suddenly he smiled, and moved to stand beside me and chat normally. I went to visit him in prison later, on a charge of GBH, a fate which befell several of our youngsters over the next few years (the prison sentence, not my visiting). I came out well from that face-off, and I learned later, with gratitude, that a Roman Catholic priest in Hulme, fulfilling the same sort of duty that same week, had been badly beaten up.

A group of bikers, thrown out from every pub, café and chip shop in a wide area, used to come in late and plan corporate disruption. By that time the technique of nipping it all in the bud had been well practised, and we had no trouble with them, fearsome as they looked. In fact, on their second or third visit, one of their number came across the room to me with a request, from a 'unanimous vote', for me to assume the role of 'Leader of the Pack'. When I had recovered from the shock I pointed out that my Lambretta was not in the same league as their lovely Honda and Kawasaki 750s and 900s, but after some to-ing and fro-ing between us I agreed to act in such a capacity and to arrange a run with them. I wrote to Allan Shaw, who was running a youth centre in the Bull Ring in Birmingham, to ask if I could take a group to visit him, a suggestion which he welcomed enthusiastically. There was a totally unexpected reaction from my 'pack' to this proposal. 'Birmingham, Vic? How far's that?'

'Oh, about ninety miles.'

Consternated silence. 'That's too far. Can we go by train?'

Stunned silence from me. 'By train?' I said eventually. 'What about the bikes?' (To say nothing of their image). Nothing more came of my one and only opportunity of large-scale biking and prestige youth leadership. I saw several of that gang over the following years, all wearing clean shirts and sitting in cars, with me still on my scooter.

'Ah well, I've got a steady girlfriend now, Vic,' was the usual embarrassed answer to my rebuke. Behind the bravado there was always a young lad growing up in a violent culture, and glad of compassion and a listening ear even if it came from a man dressed entirely in black with a dog collar.

But the macho exterior could be quite frightening. One evening the curate of Benchill, who was 'on duty' in the vicarage there (the vicar being away), waiting for possible applicants for banns of marriage or baptism, rang me out of boredom to ask if we could change places for the evening, with him taking charge of the youth activity. I was not at all convinced that it was a good idea, but I agreed. At about 9.45 p.m. I received a phone call – would I go immediately as there had been serious trouble. I arrived at the hall, which was silent and empty except for a nasty looking group of four or five lads and two girls. Walking past them with a nod, I found the curate and several of the helpers in the back room, pale and badly shaken. There had been a pitched battle between 'Mods' (scooter riders) and 'Rockers' (bikers), and the bunch in the hall were the remnants of the victorious Rockers. I went out immediately to them and said, with far more boldness than prudence, 'Right, girls, time to go home.' Only as I got closer did I notice the lead piping, the bicycle chains and the knives. But to my surprise they all turned meekly and departed. That same evening, it transpired, a Mods and Rockers battle had taken place on the south coast, which had completely wrecked a house party. We have grown more used to such social disturbances in the last forty years, but they caused great trauma across the country at that time. Towards the end of the 1960s, rock and roll was giving way to Folk, and a more gentle following of fashion took over. The routine smashing of chairs at our dances ceased abruptly. The names of the various Beatles-emulating local groups which proliferated, and upon whom we called to provide the music for these activities, were interesting. Of the thirty-odd in our acquaintance, there were the half-expected ('Dave and the Editors', 'Paul Fender and his Tigers', 'The Oddments', 'The Countdowns', 'The High-Jackers'), and the very much more unexpected ('The Troyes', 'Die Vondell', 'Talisman', 'The Web', 'The Valvolas' and 'The Zwickau Prophets', to select but a few). Truly the newly liberated teenage creative imagination of those years was not confined to the music itself.

I think the worst part of living there was having our daughter and, until he was taught self-defence (or self-offence – the Mancunian tradition was to get your retaliation in first), our son physically assaulted regularly. This was not because they were children of the vicarage; we lived in an ordinary house and half the youngsters didn't know what a vicar was anyway. It was part of the common culture. One of our neighbours saw his son being attacked one day and went out and defended him physically. This brought on the traditional retaliation – the offender's big brother (there was usually a selection of ascending sizes – in this case the biggest because the adversary was an adult). As my neighbour was a former policeman, the encounter was short-lived and the family had run out of champions.

One characteristic was groups of roving youths who threatened anyone in their way, especially children, and their behaviour was faithfully emulated by gangs of roving dogs, which went around killing cats and dogs and other pets. Jillian's rabbit was torn from its hutch and killed one dark evening in our garden. These dogs were a dire menace individually, too, on their own turf, to postmen, meter readers, vicars and other undesirable visitors. The cult of mindless cruelty and destructiveness seemed to worsen as time went on.[6] A man in his sixties who had just returned home after a heart operation was subjected to mockery and jeering from a group of ten- or eleven-year-olds, and a miner from a Manchester pit, on his way home at midnight after a late

---

[6] This was not confined to Manchester, of course, and urban violence is more widespread now than it was then. I hear, however, that Wythenshawe in the 21st century is more civilised (apart from the odd burst of gunfire) due, it is said, to the changes in housing policy and ownership.

shift, was set upon by a gang at the bus terminus and put in hospital for ten days. It was a meaningless assault, committed just for the fun of it. Another disturbing element was the dabbling of the young in such occult practices as Ouija boards, tarot cards and levitation. And not only the kids: I had a visit one morning from a distraught mother whose Ouija board had 'told' her that her ten-year-old son would be killed by a bus on his way to school on Wednesday. She didn't know which Wednesday, but we promised to pray earnestly for the lad during the next Wednesday and the one following. We heard nothing from her for over a week, but on the second Wednesday she came to the vicarage, all smiles, and told us that the boy had had a narrow escape from a double-decker bus when crossing the road near the school that morning, but he was untouched. We didn't know quite what the truth of it all was, but she was warned off such dabbling with the unknown, and all was well in the end.

Towards the end of my time there I went one evening to visit the pub with the rather less salubrious reputation of the two in the parish. To my surprise the place was full of eleven- to fifteen-year-old boys – on my previous visit it had had a 'normal' clientele. I walked over to sit among them to establish contact, but at each spot I was met with grunts and blank stares. I went to the bar and asked the licensee what was wrong with this lot.

'Don't you know?' he said. 'Look in that corner.' I followed his nod, and saw one of the lads mainlining into his thigh. That pub has been closed for several years now.

Joy had a frightening experience one evening. Coming out of the church hall after setting up for a sale of work or something similar for the following day, she was locking up when a gang appeared with a large Alsatian dog and gathered round her. They tried to get the dog to attack her, but it didn't move, so she passed calmly and safely through them and walked home. The dog, like Balaam's donkey, may have seen her guardian angel standing in front of her, and was too terrified to act.[7] The worst things I experienced personally were, first, being pelted with snowballs and insults by a gang, and on another occasion, being shot at with

---

[7] Numbers 22:21–34

a .22 rifle – the slug whirring loudly just above my head – when on my way to an 8 a.m. communion service.

I was given a lesson one evening on the psychology of 'turf-consciousness', when a curate of William Temple parish invited me to take my youth club on a visit to his young people. There was not an overwhelming response to the prospect of such a delight, but twelve or fifteen of our youngsters walked with me the few hundred or so yards to our neighbouring parish's hall. I have quite forgotten the programme that had been devised for the evening, but two things do stand out in my memory. The first was seeing, shortly after our arrival, one of our lads sitting on the edge of the stage, obviously getting to know one of the local girls very well. I tapped him on the shoulder and said, 'Come on, there's a time and a place for everything.' He replied, 'Yes. This is the time and this is the place.' I confessed to myself defeat by his presence of mind, though after I had turned away he did break off the engagement. The rest of the evening proceeded well enough, but towards 9.30 p.m. I began to feel a strange atmosphere developing and said farewell to the curate and his flock, and gathered my own together to walk home.

Soon, I became aware of a large gang of youths following us. Where they had assembled from I don't know, but I urged the kids to quicken their pace homewards while I brought up the rear. Soon, stones and pieces of wood and whatever else served as missile material helped us along imperatively. The pursuit ceased abruptly at the border between the two neighbourhoods – as clear an exposition of atavistic turf-war mentality as one could wish. I heard the next day that our pursuers had straggled back home venting their energies on lifting off all the garden gates from their hinges, and throwing them into someone else's garden.

The violence had its funny side, of course. One evening, just before we left, a young man drew up at the vicarage in an impressively huge black car, and announced himself by name, explaining that he had been one of our mid-1960s teenagers and had made good: could he take me to the pub for a drink? We went along to the more respectable of the two public houses, two hundred yards up the road, and were having a quiet getting-up-to-date when a fight broke out at the next table. Suddenly, a body flew across our table, taking the glasses and everything else with it, and slumped to the floor beyond.

'Can't have a minute's peace these days... Excuse me,' said my friend. He picked up the man from the floor, stood him on his feet and shoved him outside, locking the door behind him.

'Thanks, mate,' said the barman.

'That's OK,' replied my friend, adding to me, as he sat down again, 'Now, where were we?'

He sat there, wiping blood from his shirt and jacket. 'My wife's not going to believe that I've been having a drink with the vicar,' he said quietly.

★

> Providence, for those who believe in it, converts evil into good [...] the forces of diminishment [...] become the tool that cuts, carves, and polishes within us the stone which is destined to occupy a definite place in the heavenly Jerusalem.[8]

In 1964 the bishop of Manchester recommended that I went to the William Temple College in Rugby to attend a conference for clergy in parishes of radical social change. The conference, which was excellent, started me off on a ministry which included a strong element of social responsibility. The changing world in which we were called to witness to a timeless gospel was brought home to us vividly by an interruption of the conference: the vicar of Grantham had to leave suddenly because an engine driver at the locomotive depot there had committed suicide. The driver's world of finely honed skills, comradely teamwork and the assumed timelessness of a job on the 'permanent way' had collapsed around him and his family, on dieselisation and redundancy.

On returning home I started an informal group to discuss, as I put it in a letter of invitation in April 1965, 'the beliefs and doctrines of the Church in the light of modern developments, and under the impact of a technological world view. To work out in our parishes, with the aid of sociological techniques and disciplines, the Church's

---

[8] Pierre Teilhard de Chardin, *Le Milieu Divin*, pp.87–88.

missionary task'. To refine the point further, my next sentence read, 'A good many clergy are concerned about the effect, at parish level, of the new theology'. I invited some sixteen local clergy, of whom six attended the first meeting on 25 May, and four others (including the two Nonconformists) expressed interest. The bishop of Middleton, Ted Wickham (author of *Church and People in an Industrial City* [Sheffield]), agreed to come and give an introductory talk. We held several meetings over the next twelve months, at which point Ted Wickham told me that the dean of Manchester, Alfred Jowett, was setting up a group with similar objectives, meeting at his home. This met first on 9 July 1966. The express aims of that initiative grew out of a frustration and dissatisfaction among clergy with the conventional roles and structures of Church life, and the consequent drift of several into 'non-parochial' jobs, or away from the traditional ministry altogether into secular employment, and a similar concern among leading lay people. Of the twenty members of the group, ten were lay, mostly women but including Mark Gibbs, the author of *God's Frozen People*. The intentions of that group were stated as 'to provide a means of association for those people who have welcomed the troubling of waters in theological thinking, and to seek to work out their Christian vocation in relation to the secular world[9], and where necessary to reform the structures of the Church in accordance with this mission task'. The bishop of Middleton suggested that our local group joined with the larger one, and this we did. At this time I was a member of the Diocesan Board for Social Responsibility, becoming a member of the Executive in 1967 (and secretary of the equivalent body in the diocese of Durham when I moved there). I always held that institutions and businesses within the parish boundary were part of my pastoral responsibility, and I was listed by the Deans' Group, in December 1966, as someone 'already engaged in experimental ministry' (citing the Wythenshawe fire service, and later the police), though I remember being surprised to find that the assumption of such responsibility and 'chaplaincy' presence was cause for note.

---

[9] This was the period of numerous books on 'the death of God' theme, and the exaltation of the aims and methods of the secular city.

Several meetings of the Deans' Group took place, and at the one held in November 1966 Alfred Jowett's detailed paper was discussed, dealing with how our presentation of the Faith was no longer expressed in ways that related to a world which was rapidly changing. I replied at length, in writing, to each of his points, and in February 1967 I raised the question of clarifying the purpose and motivation of the group, because I felt that these differed among the members, and that this dissipated the discussions. Though I was broadly in sympathy with the enterprise, I had gathered fairly early on that whereas I was interested in finding better ways to communicate the timeless gospel, the thrust of the debates was more to find a new gospel. John Robinson's *Honest to God* and its sequel *But that I Can't Believe*[10] had appeared during my time in Salford, and like many theological students who had coped with Bultmann and Tillich and company, I had not thought much of it. However, those books had given widespread public credence to the severe doubts raised in academic circles as to the credibility and authority of the Bible and traditional doctrinal formulations. The reaction among lay people was that if bishops said so much was unbelievable, what chance had the ordinary person in the pew? Probably as a result of my experience of a Church-free adolescence and early adulthood, and a St Paul-like conversion, I did not have any conceptual baggage or a narrow upbringing to rebel against, and I had no problem with metaphysics, otherworldliness, miracles or angels. My concern was not with attempts to rewrite the Christian story from scratch, in concepts totally acceptable to secular thinking, but with ways of showing, in word and deed, how God as revealed in Jesus Christ, in the Old and New Testaments – progressive revelation – still had the power to change for good the lives of ordinary people and of institutions, given the chance and the trust.

I could not attend the meeting on 25 February 1967 (only nine members did so), and after that I felt that I could not go along with their proposed solution to the problem. I have described this episode in some detail because it was the harbinger of an enduring

---

[10] I tended rather to sympathise with C S Lewis, who said we should not ask 'How much of this can I accept?' but 'How much must I change in the light of what I have found?'

concern on my part for the effects of an excessively radical dismantling of the way theology and pastoral ministry had come down to us. I visualised a more reflective and deliberate evolution, in which the engine of change was the Holy Spirit, not simply human enthusiasm and reason. I was utterly convinced that orthodox theology could still have a divinising impact not only upon the Church's mission – care for members and outreach to the 'unbeliever' – but also on the secular world of structures – public services, factories, hospitals, town and county halls, government offices, colleges and schools.[11]

Joy started a Bible study group for women, which proved enormously successful, and I one for men. The latter concerned a translation of the Faith from home- and Church-base, to relationships and prayer at work. Some of the reporting back showed the Holy Spirit moving powerfully in response to prayer, in the structures and stresses of management and labour. These were greatly heartening, and perhaps the most vivid was the experience of our church treasurer, Alan Hibbert,[12] who was the production manager at Kellogg's factory in Trafford Park. That time was the era of the Militant Tendency in the Labour movement, fuelled by Marxist enthusiasm for bringing about the revolution by crippling industry with corporate non-cooperation on the part of the labour force, and Kellogg's, as a symbol of American capitalism, was a prime target. One day, the local trade union leader called an immediate strike over some tea break dispute or other. The management, including Alan, gathered a meeting together, with the union leader present, and set off a discussion of how to resolve the dispute in order to get the assembly lines moving again. The meeting was going nowhere, and the production manager was praying urgently that the Holy Spirit would take over, but an agreement seemed further off than when they started. Suddenly the door opened and the union man was told he was wanted on the phone urgently. He disappeared,

---

[11] In Wythenshawe, from the beginning, I started going regularly into the seven schools in the parish (five local authority and two Roman Catholic) on the basis of 'I will visit you regularly until you ask me not to'. I was never asked not to.

[12] Later a reader in the Chester diocese.

and though the meeting waited a while for his return, he was never seen again. God was king in industry and not only in the Church. The answer to pastoral problems presented by a society in transition, away from received and scarcely questioned certainties, was at the time being looked for by many in the Church not in the promised power of God and His sovereignty, but in organisational policies, management techniques, group therapies, psychotherapeutic counselling, stress control and the like. These things are valuable and necessary, and I used them, insofar as I had mastered them. But they were adjuncts to the answer, not the answer itself. Spiritual malaise, individual or corporate, needed spiritual remedy, and that required full recognition of the otherness of God, as well as His presence in and around us; in the power of the love of God as well as His self-limiting gift of freewill to His creatures. I could not accept a God who was as powerless in the face of human problems, whether personal or social, as we were – a theology of vague and baseless hope, and of resignation and despair rather than faith and trust. Faced with social and personal disruption, we had the choice of confronting the power of evil – that is, all rebellion against the good and perfect will of God – in the way of Jesus, as described in the Bible, or trying to cope with the problems and the distress with the aid of a message which rejected the mythological, the miraculous and the binary (material and spiritual) theology of tradition. I accepted as a package the revelation of God as given to us in the Bible, given for our guidance in the truth (and not for our intellectual frustration), to see if it worked in practice, and prepared to change my approach if it did not.

There were several seemingly intractable pastoral problems facing us early in our time in Peel Hall. One was that of a young mother diagnosed as having a life-threatening growth on her alimentary canal. We prayed passionately for her complete healing, believing that God was capable of responding. On the day appointed for her operation the surgeons found very little wrong, soon put it right, and she returned home to resume her life with husband and children. One man was officially diagnosed as a schizophrenic, and was becoming increasingly wild and threatening and facing incarceration. Enquiries by us of doctors and psychotherapists regarding his chances of recovery produced a negative prognosis. About this time I was struck by the concept of 'Novena' – a structure of nine days of concentrated prayer for a special intention. The Roman Catholic forms I examined seemed a little over-repetitious (similar to the Rosary prayers, which Joy used regularly), so I drew up a 'Scriptural Novena'. This was a sequence of scripture passages with a meditation and prayers, and it proved highly effective, and has continued to be so over the intervening forty odd years. Several people prayed for the afflicted man's complete healing. The first thing that happened was that his mother died – she had been his help and support all his life. We learned that prayer often produced such backward steps, seemingly causing worse problems before the main ones could be healed. But the man never looked back. He became normal, got a job, and worked until his retirement, and thereafter was a source of great friendship and guidance to nephews and nieces. Another stricken family had a mother who had great faith but faced, with her three young children, serious problems after her husband's father had moved in to live with them. Her husband, a very forceful ex-soldier and unbeliever, vowed he would never put his father in a home, despite the incontinence and worsening irrational behaviour. It seemed to us that the God of Jesus could not be any happier than we were in the slow deterioration of the wife, nor with advice to the effect that suffering was character building. So we set to praying fervently in the conviction that the Holy Spirit had the power to redeem the circumstances. Not long afterwards the husband, a security guard at the Bank of England in Manchester, set out one day for his lunch break, and suddenly decided to go to the Social Services offices. He went in and asked to see the top man by name (though he hadn't even known his name before then, let alone contemplated going to see him). He was told he couldn't see him without an appointment, but then was shown into the man's office to meet him anyway. The husband asked for his father to be admitted to a good old people's home; it was agreed, and within a few days he had moved into full-time care. The husband couldn't explain the sequence of events, or why he had changed his mind so completely, or how he knew where to go or whom to ask for. But he was happy he had restored well-being to his wife and children, and his father was well cared for.

With these and other similar answers to prayer a pattern was becoming established of the faithfulness of God if He was taken at His word and trusted completely. The fear of pastoral failure, or of ridicule and accusations of naivety or superstition, though real, are not worthy of faith and trust in the Judeo-Christian God. If we have no revelation to guide us, or if we are sceptical or cynical of it, then we are like highly educated and sophisticated people whose knowledge of the world and the human body are far superior to that of the ancient world, but whose understanding of God is still at the conjectural stage – hardly an advance on deism. There is a French proverb which says that 'miracles happen only to those who believe in them'.[13] We were helped in our view of faith by four books about individuals and communities who had put their heads on the block, as it were, in faith. The first was an account of a community of Lutheran Sisters which was formed in Darmstadt just before the end of the Second World War, to help build on Christian foundations once hostilities had ceased in a physically and morally ruined Germany.[14] The second book was the biography of John Vianney, the Cure D'Ars, who, despite his lack of academic ability, saw wonderful things happen in his obscure village because of his total trust in God. The third was David Wilkerson's *The Cross and the Switchblade*, a Pentecostalist minister's account of being called to preach the gospel to the warring street gangs of New York City. Finally, the fourth was the biography of another Pentecostalist preacher called Smith Wigglesworth ('God has given me a ridiculous name to keep me humble'), a Bradford plumber who had an impressive healing ministry. He was the man who, under God, kick-started the process in 1956 of 'taking the Holy Spirit into the main-line Churches' as the charismatic movement. He used to say that any

---

[13] There is also a significant passage in Matthew's Gospel to the effect that Jesus himself could not do any mighty works in the presence of lack of faith (13:57–58).
[14] Basilea Schlink, *Realities*, Zondervan Publishing House, Ninth Edition of English Translation, 1976.

prayer that was hedged around with qualifications, in case it wasn't answered, was 'a prayer of unfaith'.

The Kaleidoscope of Humanity

There were many little human joys and formative experiences in a much less 'theological' vein. Mancunians, like Liverpudlians and London East Enders, are noted for being 'characters', and I met some unforgettable ones in Wythenshawe. Three of the old men I came across in visiting were ex-boxers. Old Tommy was 'punch-drunk', and used to do the shopping for his bed-ridden wife, walking up the road shouting incomprehensible comments on the state of the world, or the weather, or Manchester United, or something. The other two had been flyweights of some note, one of whom claimed he had fought the legendary Jimmy Wilde. One old lady told me she had been in a travelling circus all her life, billed as 'The World's Strongest Woman'. It was difficult to believe, given her height (she was called 'Millichamp', but she looked much more a 'Minichamp'), but her walls were decorated with photographs, circus bills and newspaper cuttings in total verification. In one maisonette block lived a woman who was ninety-six years old and looked a strong and healthy sixty. She looked after the infirm 'elderly' in the block, and gave every appearance of being good for another twenty years. Alas, she died not long after her 100th birthday. One wife, who made a deep impression on the neighbourhood during the period when her husband was working at the airport, was a Muslim woman of striking appearance. She was tall and dignified, and was never seen in any garment except a gown-like dress of pale blue. When I visited her, she explained how she bathed before each of the five prayer times every day, and her grace and calm encouraged me to ask for her prayers from time to time for the parish. Her presence at the school gates each day impressed the other mothers so much that several of them spoke of her as a trusted confidante and friend. Three members of the congregation and their families came under the heading of 'extraordinary'. Our first two organists in Peel Hall were teenagers. Simon Parker – actually a violinist – was a devoted admirer of Sir John Barbirolli, conductor of the Halle Orchestra, even to the hairstyle. He left us after a couple of years to pursue his higher education and was replaced by an even younger but equally competent boy called Philip Chapman, who was not yet fifteen when he was appointed. He too left us for higher education and was replaced by Don Whalley, a sign writer of church and other noticeboards and Eddie Stobart lorries. The accomplishment of the two youngsters verged on the astonishing, given their cultural environment. A near neighbour of Philip was the head of our Sunday school from the outset, Helen Pelmear. She was in her early twenties, and gave devoted service to our children. Her mother had been a nun, and her father was a scientific humanist.[15] The eldest son of the family, aged twenty-six, was a digger of holes in the road for the electricity board, but in his leisure hours read philosophy. He had an incredible grasp of seriously knotty texts, and I lent him some of my books and asked for his résumé of them later. One of these was a theological work, *The Mind and the Heart of Love*, by Martin D'Arcy, a text which I myself had found difficult. His 'seminar' showed that he had a sound understanding of it. I asked him why he was not pursuing his education to higher levels (he had left school without any qualifications), but he replied that he was quite happy with his life as it was.

I visited an old lady ('old' as in eighty-three, but she had the face of a lovely fifty-year-old), too infirm with heart trouble to leave her bed, and becoming impossibly overweight because of it. During the course of our conversation she suddenly said, 'If Jesus were to walk through that door now, he would heal me.'

While I was carefully considering my response, her sixteen-year-old great-granddaughter walked in. So, after a few minutes, I prayed with and blessed her and left – the theological problem still unaddressed. Not long after that I was in the house of a churchwarden whose wife was ill. As I was leaving, he said to me, 'If Jesus were to walk through the door now, he would heal her.'

I was so taken aback at the verbatim repetition that again I did not respond. But I resolved privately that if it happened again I would take action immediately, on the grounds that Jesus was

---

[15] Though he, like others, asked me to read the Bible to him, and to expound it for him, when he was dying.

there: he had given power and commandment to his Church to heal the sick, promising that we would 'do greater things than he', and that ordination conferred such authority over the powers of darkness.

It was not until some time later, when I had moved to another parish, when the next repetition occurred. The first confirmation class included not only eleven- and twelve-year-olds, but practically all the children in the village aged seven and above.[16] One of the actual candidates for confirmation in the current year was a lad who spent a lot of time off school because of asthma. Part way through a class, as we were discussing Jesus' ministry, he suddenly said, 'If Jesus were to walk through that door now, he would heal me.'

That was it, I thought. I asked him to stay behind after the class and walked home with him, explaining what I was going to do. I put it to his parents (non-churchgoers) that I would like to have, in response to what the lad had said, a service of prayer, anointing and laying on of hands for the boy's healing. They agreed and we fixed a date and, having in the meantime surrounded them with prayers, we held the ceremony in their house. The lad's asthma cleared up, and he enjoyed a trouble-free stretch of schooling thereafter.

I had decided, very soon after ordination, that my function as a priest was to work towards making myself redundant, on the grounds of 'every member ministry': the belief that God called each member of the Church to his or her own specific ministry. (This would obviously exclude the functions which defined a priest – blessing, absolving and consecrating). Although I held to that ideal throughout, there was no escaping the fact that leadership, if it is to focus, interpret and coordinate all discussion and endeavour, involves helping the 'people committed to one's cure and charge'[17] to reach a common mind and action. It means exhibiting a comprehensive grasp of the problems and subjects facing the Christian family in the parish or deanery, and equip-

---

[16] The youngest had attended every year for four years by the time she was confirmed.

[17] 1928 *Book of Common Prayer* ordination service.

ping oneself in holy wisdom to provide counsel, sympathy and advice where it is needed. I don't suppose I measured up well in all these spheres, but I was convinced always that God was with me in all my efforts. The members of our three main congregations in Peel Hall – Methodist, Roman Catholic and Anglican – were indeed shining lights (for the most part!) in the parish. The awareness of being 'up against it' in the general cultural milieu made it important that the three congregations kept in touch with each other. The Roman Catholic priest, Louis St John, was a saint by any standards. He served sixteen years in Wythenshawe as a curate of St John Benchill and then as parish priest of St Elizabeth's Peel Hall, and going from there to a similar (Liverpool overspill) estate in Runcorn, only to suffer a near nervous breakdown there.[18] The Methodist minister changed every three years or so because of stress – the church and Manse were at the Civic Centre – but did magnificent work while they were with us. The Roman Catholic presbytery house was quite near the vicarage, and Louis would often drop in, in the late afternoon, to play with our children before going home.

I had initiated a 'Church Visitors' scheme, a modification of the more usually-named 'Street Warden' system, which I had learned from Richard Palmer in Salford. Each area of the parish would be under the watchful eyes of a church member, who delivered a copy of the parish magazine each month to all who regularly wanted one, and had spare copies to use as a 'calling card', or as an excuse to visit any house where there was distress of any kind or sickness, reporting back to the incumbent when someone needed a priestly visit. This worked quite well, and when one of the team reported to us, at the monthly meeting, that the adjacent parish of Heald Green (in the Chester diocese) had started a 'Community

---

[18] It had been a sad mistake to make him serve in yet another vast municipal housing estate. He said that the Church of England had been wise to transfer the Wythenshawe development to Manchester diocese from the diocese of Chester, and his Church would have done well to have taken it into the diocese of Salford. 'To the bishop of Shrewsbury diocese,' he said, 'a housing estate was three bungalows on the edge of a village.' He was, however, transferred from Runcorn to Ashton on Mersey, Sale, in Cheshire, and finally to the pleasant village of Marple.

Care' scheme, and raised the question of our doing something similar, the idea was warmly received. An important function of the parish church was to build up a sense of community, irrespective of church denomination or attitude to religion, and thus it was obvious to us that such a scheme, while continuing our system of Church Visitors, would have to be interdenominational.

The first meetings of a committee formed to establish the possibilities were very interesting. We had a fair representation of people from the three congregations, and for many of them it was their first 'official' face-to-face with Christians of another denomination. This was especially true of those who had come from Nonconformist or Low Anglican churches and had grave misgivings and misunderstandings about Roman Catholic priests, and Louis himself had never experienced such blunt and sometimes rather hostile questions. The development of these community-centred activities was attended by a growth of recognition by other local officials and organisations: our MP (Alf Morris, Minister for the Disabled), town councillors, the police and so on. We were sometimes taken for a ride by men who aligned themselves with our endeavours, apparently assuming our impartial concern for the welfare of the community, gaining popular credence, and then setting themselves up for election as town councillors at the first opportunity, and distancing themselves from our 'amateur' efforts. But we were succeeding in showing that the gospel was not confined to religion but was concerned with human wholeness. One memorable example of the scheme's effectiveness was when we mounted an opposition to the proposed building of another public house in the parish. The proposed site had been allocated to a brewery at the planning stage of the estate, and was very near to one and not far from the other of the two existing pubs. We were unanimous in not wanting another punch-up centre in our midst. We got to know the time and date of the hearing in the magistrates' court in Manchester, and organised the hire of a double-decker bus, and fifty-odd people to attend. Many of them were young mothers, and we encouraged them to bring their toddlers and babes as outward and visible signs of our concern. The brewer's legal counsel put forward the formal proposal, and our solicitor responded with our objections. When the proposer started to argue the case, the children – seemingly with one accord – kicked up such an enormous and sustained racket that, despite our apologies to the magistrate (accepted), the brewer's solicitor suddenly announced his client's withdrawal of the application for a licence entirely, and we all went home rejoicing.[19] From this scheme grew the Ratepayers' Association which met regularly in our church hall.

Having declared myself in this ecumenical venture, I ought to record how, during my whole ministry, I had appreciated the benefit of being a representative of the established Church. It made a great difference at 'ground level'. Visiting door-to-door on a new housing estate makes an impression on almost everyone, whatever their church allegiance or attitude to religion. Once, I met the Baptist minister from Newall Green on the same exercise, and he mentioned ruefully the advantages we enjoyed.

'They reply to my introduction of myself by saying immediately that they are Methodist or Roman Catholic or Church of England or whatever, and close the door,' he said. 'I suppose they say to you, "Oh, come in vicar," no matter what they are!'

This was quite true – with rare exceptions. One of these exceptions was when I visited a man whom the Church Visitors' scheme had thrown up as having been diagnosed as terminally ill. Before I could speak, he looked me up and down and said, 'What the b— h— do you want?'

When I explained, he asked me in with great reluctance, and I visited him regularly over the remaining six or so months of his life. When he became bedfast he wanted me to read the Bible to him on each visit. Similar things happened on other occasions too, where a riding of verbal punches and responses they hadn't expected led to a trust in confidence and a closer walk with God.

But the great joy of working together with Christians of other denominations was to see age-old hostilities gradually melting away. Manchester wasn't quite like Belfast or Glasgow, or even

---

[19] The site was adopted, after receiving assurance that we did not need it, by Fr Louis, and the Roman Catholic church of St Elizabeth was eventually built there.

Liverpool, in the chasm between Roman Catholics and others. But with over a third of the population of the parish being at least nominally Roman Catholics[20] there was far more feeling on both sides than in most other parts of the country. Seeing in practice Louis St John's openness and obvious goodness, and the respect with which he and I treated each other, people began to trust him, and to see his flock with different eyes. We got to a certain degree of shared ministry. For example, he used to ask me to visit some of his flock ('Will you go and see Mrs X – she's on Top Doh again, and you're much better with the women than I am'), and after I had left the parish he visited our housebound people until my successor arrived.

In 1970 the Whit Walks of Witness, traditionally a show of strength between Anglicans and Roman Catholics in Manchester and South Lancashire – one on the Monday in Whit Week and the other on the following Friday – became integrated. This led to the loss of the competitively-minded Paisleyites on our side and the Ultra-Montanes[21] on the other. But it was a great step forward, and made a great difference.

During those last three years of my time in Wythenshawe, new initiatives and new developments presented themselves. I was asked to organise a festival of arts and crafts to take place in the civic centre. The detailed organisation of the event was taken over very early by one of the curates of William Temple parish, whose church, having been built on the boundary of the parish, opposite the civic centre, had assumed the role of 'civic church'. That parish seemed to have at the time a succession of very able and sociable curates, and the arts and crafts festival 'Impact 70' was certainly enthusiastically and efficiently organised, and received great participation from local talent. 'Wythenshawe is regarded by many as a cultural and spiritual wilderness,' wrote the local historian, Derick Deakin in 1984,[22] 'and yet here in the influence

---

[20] Of a total population of over 9,500, some 3,200 were Roman Catholic. The footballing colour allegiances were the opposite of Liverpool's – red for 'Catlicks' and blue for 'Prodidogs'.
[21] My classification, not their own!
[22] In *Wythenshawe: The Story of a Garden City*, vol.2, p.216.

of the churches can be found a commitment rarely seen elsewhere.'

Justification by Faith

A seminal experience just before I left theological college had been a visit by Dr Frank Lake, a missionary doctor who, from his studies in theology and psychotherapy, had devised a course of 'clinical theology', a modern presentation of the doctrine of justification by faith. We are all conditioned from childhood to desire acceptance and approbation from parents or guardians and teachers and so on, but most of the time in the process of learning to relate to the world and our own self-awareness we need our faults and misunderstandings correcting. The constant message of 'Don't do that', 'Stop it', 'Do as you are told, or else' and sometimes 'You are so stupid', impose the message that we must try harder, because we are not good enough as we are, giving us the impression of being utterly and completely unacceptable. This can lead to self-disgust, despair and guilt. The desire to get into favour with figures of authority can be transferred to our relationship with God. He is, we are told, perfect and wishes us to be perfect in everything. And so we strive to please Him by good deeds and a neurotic compulsion to the achievement of perfection. Or the conviction of worthlessness can lead to rage, rebellion, and the discarding of all attempts to please and to conform to norms and expectations. Once we have developed a mode of living with ourselves, and the challenges and pressures from the world and other people, any threat to that composure has to be met with a counter-attack. This we can renounce in the peace and acceptance born of the realisation that God is the judge of our shortcomings, not others, and we can accept criticism if it has truth, and hand it over to God if it has not. God accepts us just as we are, and the principle extends to relationships between persons, too. We are to accept them as they are, without expecting them to agree with us. When they offend us, we do not demand higher standards than we deliver to them, but are accepting and understanding. It is built into all of us, high or low, to demand perfection of others in the way they treat us, while being quite aware of our own, unadmitted, imperfections.

St Paul makes clear that we are justified (that is, made 'just' and 'not guilty') by trusting in God as revealed in Jesus, not by being regarded as perfect at keeping rules and directives, wherever they originate from.[23] Thus we do not have to become 'religious', in the usual sense of term, to be right with God. The key text is Jesus' Parable of the Prodigal Son,[24] which illustrates the attitude of God to those of us (all of us in some way and at some times) who rebel against His authority and His demands, to go off to follow our own selfish ways. Helmut Theilicke, the great German preacher and theologian of the post-1945 moral and economic reconstruction of his country, suggested that the parable should be called 'The Parable of the Waiting Father'. God, like a loving father, waits for us to return to Him with love and affection and accepts us back with a complete lack of condemnation. Jesus showed us on the cross that He accepted our guilt, our shortcomings, our deliberate sins when repented of and has obtained our forgiveness and restoration by the Father. He has done this irrespective of our failings to 'measure up', and our pitiful and unnecessary attempts to win His favour. 'We have all fallen short', said St Paul; but when we 'arise and go back to the father' he receives us without judgement or punishment. This doctrine of justification by faith, and not by deeds of appeasement of guilt, became my bedrock of resort, whenever my numerous failings in ministry and in family responsibilities assailed my self-confidence. Ultimately, our self-respect, our proper functioning, rests not on ourselves but on Jesus' reconciling work. Many people understandably turn to 'religion' to quell their feelings of inadequacy. Religion, with its codes and rules, gives them somewhere to hide from their feelings of unworthiness, and if it leads them eventually to find the Truth as it is in Christ, all can be well. But so often it leads them to self-justification and to divide everyone else into 'goodies and baddies', and to treat other people with disdain, contempt or even hatred, thus making a mockery of the God who became man to reconcile all humankind to himself and to each other. As against such 'religion', God accepts the

---

[23] The Epistle to the Romans, 5:1–7; to the Galatians 3, etc. Of course God wants us to be good, but he doesn't wait until we are perfect before he accepts us and loves us.

[24] St Luke's Gospel, Chapter 15.

unworthy, the outcast, the failures, looking upon them as seen in Jesus. William Bright, in his Eucharistic hymn, 'And now, O Father, mindful of the love / Which bought us once for all on Calvary's Tree' expressed it well in the second verse: 'Look Father, look on his anointed face / And only look on us as found in him'. God sees us not as we feel ourselves to be, but as a beloved child, loved as in Jesus, His beloved Son.

Most parishes have their share of phlebotically-minded parochial church council members – those who regard it as their vocation and ministry to oppose their incumbent at every opportunity. It was a great relief to me one day, during the Morning Office, to realise that even Jesus had one such person in his leadership team. If the divine proportion was one in twelve, then perhaps we are sharing in his ministry in that way, too. (And there's some consolation, also, in the way an oyster produces pearls!) There were times when the opposition from people who were in trusted positions in the Christian family caused great stress.[25] At such periods, it was a restoration of trust in God to come, at evening prayer of the seventh day of the month (using the system of reading the Psalms daily in the *Book of Common Prayer*), to Psalm 37:

> Fret not thyself because of the ungodly [...] for they shall soon be cut down like the grass [...] Put thy trust in the Lord, and be

---

[25] One of the 'opposition' sources, surprisingly, was the lay reader, John Tricket, who, during the second year of my time in Peel Hall, committed himself to our mission from being one of the several readers in Heald Green, the neighbouring parish in the Chester diocese. He was the Head Master of Sharston School, in Benchill parish, and a great help and support he was: a down-to-earth South Yorkshire man from Conisborough, near Mexborough, and a committed Christian in his job as well as at church. He used to sit on the back row of the PCC and make blunt counter-proposals to mine on every subject under discussion. I wondered at this apparent lack of support for a while, but one day an explanation came to me. In his work, in a school of 1,200 pupils, his was the desk where the buck stopped, and every Monday of the week was taken up entirely by the staff having to restore at least one of the buildings to workable condition, having been wrecked over the weekend. PCC Meetings were a place where someone else was in the hot seat, and someone else had the final responsibility. He could be the rebel on the back row of seats. I felt happy after that to take the brunt of his emotional needs. He invariably voted in the right way when it came to the crunch.

doing good. Dwell in the land, and verily thou shalt be fed […]
Hold thee still in the Lord, and abide patiently upon him.[26]

In about the middle of the 1960s, the need for a parish stewardship campaign made itself felt. The immediate reaction of the PCC to the suggestion was to be against it (with two or three exceptions). It was discussed several times at later meetings, some very attractive literature was produced by our church wardens and treasurer, and we invited a diocesan adviser to address the PCC. He seemed rather to strengthen the opposition than persuade it, but the time came for a meeting when a decisive vote had to be taken. In my prayers, I figured that if God wanted us to have a healthy commitment to stewardship of our personal income and resources, then it was up to Him to move hearts and minds in favour. And if He did not, then we had no cause to be asking for it.

The treasurer (not the same man as previously mentioned in that office) came to see me on the afternoon before the crucial meeting. 'Do you realise that very few of the PCC are going to vote in favour this evening?' he asked, anxiously. I replied as above, broadly, and assured him that the Holy Spirit was in charge; and there was no need for me to whiz round everybody trying to persuade them against their doubts, and asked him to turn his anxiety into extra knee drill. The discussion at the meeting was every bit as unpromising as the treasurer had foretold. I entered a final silent plea to the Holy Spirit as I asked for a show of the twenty-seven or twenty-eight hands. The vote, apart from one abstention, was unanimously in favour. Several of the previously opposed members said afterwards that they did not know why they had voted as they did. They had gone to the meeting resolute in their determination to vote against it. The campaign was highly successful. The Devil (or whatever we call the undeniable presence of the force of evil in the world if we want to personify it) had a happy hunting ground in the area; but there were many times and events in which he was roundly frustrated. That was one of them. But the most prominent of them centred on the building of the new church.

---

[26] 'Be still; and know that I am God' (Psalm 46:10) needs to be our constant reminder that, whatever our responsibilities, we are not totally responsible – He is.

The late 1960s was a bleak time theologically for embarking on such a project. The construction of a building set apart solely for God, instead of affirming that He was present in the everyday and everywhere, was losing ground. A secular Christianity was the flavour of the time, and spending money on buildings which would be used for only twenty or so hours a week was too traditional, locked in the past, too opposed to current theological trend, and in general far too contrary to current ecclesiological thinking to be entered into without searching questions. Among the 'in' books at the time were *God is No More* by Werner Pelz (a parish priest in Salford) and his wife Lotte; *The Secular City* by Harvey Cox; and several with variations on the theme of 'God is Dead' (notably by Thomas Altizer). I would have been the last to deny that the God of Abraham, Moses and Elijah, and Jesus the Christ was present in the whole world and all that is in it (those books were actually very helpful).[27] But there was the undeniable and irreplaceable theology of 'Come apart and rest awhile' – the need for spiritual peace and renewal in an all-too-worldly everyday life which did not often enough reveal its spiritual dimension; and an enduring conviction of the existence of a Creator who is personal but ineffable, beyond and above, beneath and behind, the stress and violence of each day, who cares whether we are happy or not.

It was a debate we had in PCC and other gatherings, and our consensus was that although God could be found everywhere, the idea of 'holy ground', holy space set apart for God alone, was deeply engrained in the human heart. After all, though all our time is God's, we set aside certain times in the week especially for Him; all our money and possessions belong to Him, but we give him a proportion as a symbol of that truth. So, our argument went, God is everywhere but we dedicate some space to Him alone as a symbol of His presence. Additional practical impetus was given to the argument by the fact that the atmosphere and

---

[27] The 'god' of those writers, as with John Robinson in *Honest to God* and its sequels, was the one spoken of by Nietzsche, the death of whom he foretold, because by his time the word 'god' 'had deteriorated into a package concept for a multitude of abstract and abstruse, pious and impious aspirations' (Pelz). It was unarguably time to dethrone that one.

smell of the weekday activities, and especially Saturday's bazaars and jumble sales in our all-purpose hall, carried over into Sunday. Although incense was used in the early Church in the catacombs of Rome and had the effect, it is reported, of counteracting such distractions, it was not really an option in the minds of a congregation who had been rehoused from Low, Middle or Evangelical parishes, with only a sprinkling used to a Catholic tradition. In view of all these considerations, a new building it was. The requisite permission was obtained from the diocese (we had been in a 'conventional district' – a parish area without a consecrated purpose-built church – since May 1965),[28] and a date was fixed for a ground-breaking ceremony. Providentially, enough ground was available on the end of the site of the dual-purpose building, and the plan was to construct the new building as interconnected with it.

The proposed dedication of the church was a subject of interesting discussions. The hall had been known as All Saints, a name chosen by the vicar of Benchill because, as a curate, he had met his wife at a church of that dedication. This proved not to be completely suitable: there were five other churches of that dedication within five miles (plus the nearby Roman Catholic school of All Hallows), and our bills and payments were going astray. The debate spread over two or three PCC meetings, and as nearly everyone had come from a different parish, each put forward the one they knew best, and agreement proved to be difficult. Somebody suggested the name of St George, a scarcely veiled assertion of C of E-ism in a parish with a very large Roman Catholic presence. That was not thought to be a worthy idea, and so it was agreed that we should appeal to the bishop, presenting him with a summary of our discussions and a shortlist for his decision. Thus we arrived at St Richard of Chichester, suggested

---

[28] The 'progression' was curate of Benchill, Wythenshawe (priest in charge of the Peel Hall area), September 1963 to April 1965; curate in charge of the conventional district of All Saints Peel Hall, May 1965 to November 1969; minister in charge of the ecclesiastical district of St Richard of Chichester, Wythenshawe, November 1969 to 1971, and vicar from 1971 to 1973. An 'ecclesiastical district' was a parish with a consecrated church but not yet full legal status as a parish (we had moved too fast for the legal processes).

because the Sunday school, during its years of occupation of the hall, had always concluded its sessions with the Prayer of St Richard. This was appropriate also in that all the post-war new churches in Wythenshawe had been given more imaginative dedications than 'St Mary' or 'St John' – St Martin, St Francis, William Temple – and Benchill parish church itself, built just before the War, was 'St Luke the Physician', rather than the usual 'St Luke the Evangelist'.

The date we had arranged for the ground breaking was 3 April 1969, Maundy Thursday and the Feast Day of St Richard. Our oldest member, Mrs Ibbotson, well into her nineties, was furnished with a silver spade (painted by me for the occasion), and a specially written ceremony was performed in the presence of thirty or forty people. An architect was recommended by the diocese – an assistant organist at the cathedral and of an architectural practice well-experienced in building churches. He was Gordon Thorne, of Hately, Winterbottom and Thorne of Manchester, and a first-rate appointment in all respects it turned out to be. Ever since my incarceration for ten months in a sanatorium with an architect studying for his final examinations, I had developed a great interest for the subject and, over the next few months, Gordon and I had many discussions on architecture and on theology, over draft drawings and detail fittings and on faith and its implications. Gordon chose a builder with whom he had worked well before – J Jarvis and Sons Ltd of Sale – and preparation work was started on 16 June 1969, the Feast of the Translation of St Richard.[29] The foundation stone, a part of Manchester Cathedral blown off in the Blitz of 1940, was laid by the bishop of Hulme[30] on 21 June. Stones from four other cathedrals were built into the walls, as symbolic of the fact that this was but the latest development in a long process of witness to God's presence in the affairs of mankind in that area. They were from the cathedrals of Chichester, Chester (Wythenshawe was in that diocese before 1933), of Lichfield (in which diocese it was

---

[29] This feast marks the removal of his body to Chichester Cathedral from Dover where he had died.
[30] Kenneth Venner Ramsey, bishop of Hulme from 1953 to 1975.

Foundation stone, part of Manchester Cathedral, blown off in the Blitz of 1940.

before 1547), and the altar mensa and plinths were from York Minster, the cathedral church of the province. My theological college, St Aidan's, had closed on 26 June that year after preparing men for ordination for 123 years, and it was a great joy to be able to incorporate the bell and the suspended cross over the altar from the college chapel in our new building.[1]

The consecration of the church was scheduled for All Saints Day, 1 November 1969. The quotation of this date in answer to various questioners caused widespread incredulity and scepticism at the expense of my naivety (I wasn't absolutely sure of it myself, except as a matter of faith!). There was ample cause for such doubts. The public house up the road, recently completed, had its central heating system installed three times, because the first two were dismantled and taken away overnight. Barrowloads of bricks and cement disappeared without trace and had to be replaced each time. The final cost of that pub was rumoured to be one and a half times the initial estimate of about £137,000. The diocese advised us to enquire about the engagement of a night watchman and guard dog on our site, but £73 a week was well beyond us. So we decided that we would call on divine assistance (after all, we were doing it for Him), and pray that St Michael and all his angels would safeguard our flimsy perimeter railing, which covered only half the site anyway. During the whole period we lost only a few bricks which had fallen off a high pile against the railings and onto the public pavement. The doubters were confounded, and the site foreman was dumbfounded when he totted up the complete lack of theft, vandalism and, best of all, the total absence of illness, accident and industrial unrest among his team during the whole contract. Not only was the church finished within eighteen weeks and ready four days before the appointed date for the consecration, but the total cost came out under the budget of £25,000.[2]

An enormous amount of prayer on the part of a large number

---

[1] The chapel organ proved to be too expensive to move and install.
[2] I learned many years later that this, the last parish to be formed in Wythenshawe, thus echoed the building of the first new parish in 1937. St Michael and All Angels, Lawton Moor, designed to an almost unique (only one other in the world) star-shaped plan, was built in an atmosphere of close friendship between architect, builder and incumbent, and for less than the estimated cost of £10,000.

of people lay behind these facts, and God had clearly responded. The folk of St Richard's were indeed 'saints' in the true sense: they had to be to cut so vividly across the culture in which they lived, and to interpret all the setbacks over the years as being within the overall providence of their Lord. The pews were constructed by our church men, under the able guidance of the practically-gifted church wardens, Philip Symond and Tom Roach, the large-scale trimming and planing being prepared as a woodwork project by the lads of Sharston School. The kneelers were worked by the church women, and the altar drape, donated by Gordon Thorne, was fashioned by a parishioner. The church was duly consecrated on Saturday 1 November by the bishop of Manchester, and the following day, after the very first Eucharist at 8 a.m., the architect came running out in tears. I asked him what had happened and he replied, 'I have been struck by lightning!' This was a reference to the conclusion of one of our long discussions about faith. He said he thought he would have to be struck by lightning to believe as I had described during our travels. That Sunday morning's events were a wonderful conclusion to the whole exercise. Gordon, a gentleman of nature and of grace, was a pleasure to work with, and he contributed generously of his own time and money throughout.[3] He was responsible particularly for the choice, and the installation, of the new organ – a former recital instrument at Manchester Cathedral, rebuilt and

---

[3] A native of Lancashire, Gordon worked on many restoration works in several churches in the Manchester diocese after gaining a distinction in his final architectural thesis. These included major work on St Mark, Worsley (George Gilbert Scott's first church) and All Saints Stand (Charles Barry's first church). He was the Chairman of the Diocesan Committee for the care of buildings for five years and, as well as St Richard's, he designed the new church of St Aidan, Lower Kersal. He was also responsible for designing churches in the Roman Catholic dioceses of Nottingham, Salford and Leeds.

He started to play the organ as a choirboy at Stand parish church, where he has played over the last fifty-six years, and studied the instrument with Dr Francis Jackson at York Minster. He has given recitals at many cathedrals including York, Norwich, Canterbury, Manchester, Liverpool, Blackburn and St David's and, having a special interest in the 20th century repertoire, has commissioned two major works from the composer John McCabe. He was organ adviser to the dioceses of Manchester (1974–86) and Blackburn (1983–93) and was cathedral architect at Blackburn from 1983 to 1993. In 2005 he was awarded the Cross of St Augustine by the archbishop of Canterbury for services to the Church.

mounted on the inside wall above the entrance to the worship space.

It was too much to expect that the forces of evil, the 'principalities and powers of the universe' referred to by St Paul, would accept all these events lying down. On the following Sunday I arrived at the church to find that someone had killed a hare and spread its blood all over the entrance. Nine or so weeks later, when our first guest preacher, the bishop of Middleton, Ted Wickham, arrived, we found that the whole door and porchway were covered in an orange paint. When I apologised to him, he said simply, 'What do you expect? This is Wythenshawe!' The niggling and sniping were to be a feature of the building for some time afterwards, and the favourite trick over the years was having someone set fire to the oil-heating tank.

During the first month I had a visit from a fellow member of the Executive of the Diocesan Board for Social Responsibility. He wanted to know what we had done, and to have an explanation for why someone, whose concern for society as a whole exceeded by far his interest in churchiness, should nevertheless have entered into spending time and energy and money on a specially set-aside building. On our way to the church he pointed out the accepted arguments in favour of shared space for 'secular' activities and worship, and was still in mid flow when we entered the inner door of the church. He stopped suddenly as the atmosphere hit him. It was cool and quiet and with a feeling of (there's no other word) holiness. He said simply, 'No. I see now what you mean.' We had built it without windows, the light coming, quite copiously, from bonnets in the flat roof. This was partly to avoid the entertainment of half-bricks crashing through wall-windows during 'Onward Christian Soldiers',[4] but partly also to avoid the distraction of big red Manchester buses and other traffic passing the windows. The effect on the interior really was inspiring. We had several visits from parishes and schools during the next two or three years.

---

[4] Though the lads from the secondary school round the corner soon rose to the challenge: within a fortnight, through sheer persistence, one of the main lights in the main bonnet was cracked.

A very personal experience of mine ought to be mentioned in connection with the new building. Much of the inspiration to trust the Third Person of the Holy Trinity for all our work begun, continued and ended in Him, had come from my meeting a Pentecostal lay preacher at the Methodist Young People's club after I had come out of hospital (he was the boyfriend of one of the girls at the church). As I was at the time a *tabula rasa* and a complete neophyte I was very impressed by their reliance on God's Spirit (that he was not living in retirement, which was the impression sometimes given by mainstream Christian bodies, having been supplanted by human reason at the Enlightenment). Particularly of interest was their emphasis on what they called 'Baptism in the Holy Spirit with signs following', majoring on Acts 2:4, 8, 14–18, and I Corinthians 12:10.

After fourteen years of having the subject very much on the back burner, it came back to me that I should pray for our new church to be filled with the Holy Spirit, so that worshippers and visitors could know more closely for themselves His presence and power; and I myself, too, if God willed such a thing. I realised that religious 'experiences' were certainly not part of my genetic inheritance of over six hundred years of hard-headed Yorkshire land agents, and was aware of Bishop Joseph Butler's rebuke to John Wesley in Bristol in August 1739: 'Sir, the pretending to extraordinary revelations and gifts of the Holy Ghost is a horrid thing, a very horrid thing'. But I realised also that our ministry is not unalterably determined by any human culture, but is at the disposal of the Creator Spirit of the universe; and that it was at least possible He might have surprises and unthinkable joys in store.

So it was that after our services on our new church's first Good Friday[5] I stayed in church for a while to give thanks and to pray. I don't know how long I was there, kneeling at the marble altar rail, before I became aware of a huge 'breathing' sound, as if I were inside a lung. It grew stronger, and I had to tell myself to keep calm and receptive. Opening my eyes slightly I saw the marble tiles of the sanctuary floor heaving like sea waves, and hurriedly closed them again. My own breathing seemed to

---
[5] 27 March 1970.

synchronise with it. After a while, all returned to quietness as before, except that I felt a remarkable calmness and peaceful elevation. I went home and told Joy what had happened[6] and later, having just gone to bed, going over in my mind the events of the day, I was suddenly overwhelmed with a feeling of love for God, and started to express it in words I couldn't understand. The gift of 'speaking in tongues' is controversial, and before it was commended by David Duplessis, the representative of the Pentecostalist churches to the World Council of Churches meeting in South Africa[7] in 1956, it was more or less confined to the so-called 'full gospel' churches. Since then the 'charismatic experience' has become not uncommon (though mostly unobtrusively) in the mainstream denominations. In more recent years it accrued some disrepute because of many instances of antinomianism and unbalanced theological judgement, but as a Biblical injunction it is of great value in prayer when our own words are hard to find, and as an ever-present reminder of God's blessings. It also fulfils its original function of conveying God's will, to willing hearers, through speakers who are humble enough to commit themselves to messages which are beyond their own intellectual insights. Such a gift does not impart infallibility or even, necessarily, high holiness. But it is helpful to read Joseph Ratzinger's view of the charismatic movement: 'It is evidence of hope, a positive sign of the times, a gift of God to our age. It is a rediscovery of the joy and wealth of prayer over against theories and practices which had become increasingly ossified and shrivelled as a result of secularised rationalism'.[8]

Of great support during those hectic years, and afterwards, was the reading of the lives and writings of the great saints and

---

[6] She had a similar experience not long after, in the chapel at St Peter's Convent Horbury, near Wakefield, where she was on retreat. Another retreatant was in the chapel at the time, and she heard Joy breathing heavily – 'like a woman in labour', as she put it. Joy said later, that as a Midwife and Health Visitor, she had had trouble with the doctrine of the Virgin Birth, but had no difficulty at all after that experience!

[7] At the instigation of the preacher Smith Wigglesworth, see p.51.

[8] In 'The Ratzinger Report', 1984, summarising twenty years of the influence of the Second Vatican Council.

'warriors of the faith'. I would particularly mention (choosing from very many) Thomas a Kempis, C S Lewis, William Temple, the anonymous *The Way of a Pilgrim* (and the use in Orthodox spirituality of the 'Jesus Prayer' as a mantra in meditation), Staretz Silouan, Richard Wurmbrandt, Mother Julian of Norwich, Rudolph Otto's *The Idea of the Holy*, Teilhard de Chardin and the Orthodox writer Tito Colliander (his *Way of the Ascetics* is not for the faint-hearted, though written by a lay Christian for laypersons).[9]

In 1971 I was invited to become a 'lecturer' for the Archbishops' Committee on Evangelism. The system was that we would pay a carefully pre-planned visit to any parish which had appealed to the Committee for help in spiritual and social revitalisation. After a plenary conference in York in March 1972, the first one I was involved in, together with Peter Akehurst, vicar of St James's, Didsbury,[10] was a large housing estate of about 24,000 people in Hull. Our preliminary visit made us aware that not only that parish but every parish in the city except one was suffering acutely from serious problems – social *ennui*, ministerial burnout and theological depression. I don't know what ameliorative effect we had. Our next assignment was to have been in Workington, in Carlisle diocese, in mid-1973, but my imminent departure from Manchester diocese prevented any planning visits, and after that I seemed to become 'lost' from that particular system. I, at least, was slightly anxious in such exercises in case we were questioned too closely about the level of success we were achieving in our own parishes![11]

Certain attempts which might have come under such scrutiny were initiated during those later years. In October 1971 a Parish Fellowship was formed, by the conflation of my Men's Bible

---

[9] Oxford: Mowbray's, 1983.
[10] Who had previously been Director of Church Expansion in the diocese of Bloemfontein, South Africa.
[11] Rather as in the episode of the old Scottish farmer who mentioned to a friend that he was expecting an advisory visit from an agricultural specialist. When asked who the specialist was, he replied that he was, 'a farmer from about fifty miles away'. Upon which the friend commented, 'I see. A specialist is someone just like us, but coming from a sufficient distance'.

Group and Joy's Women's Bible Study (which comprised some twenty-eight members, most of whom went on the retreats she organised once a year). In 1968 a Young Peoples' Fellowship had been established, after my most successful confirmation class, when I led sixteen youngsters on a course based on the recently released *Sergeant Pepper's Lonely Hearts Club Band* LP. It was surprising how adaptable to points of Christian doctrine and real-life teenage ethics most of the tracks proved themselves to be. From the emphasis on love ('A Little Help from my Friends') to the empty escapism of drugs ('Lucy in the Sky with Diamonds') to trying to treat other people better ('It's Getting Better'), these songs proved to have a real impact. From this group there developed in 1972 a Junior Parochial Church Council. This was elected by the young people in the Fellowship and the confirmed members of the uniformed organisations including Guides, Brownies, Cub Scouts, Church Lads' Brigade and Church Girls' Brigade. These were all enormous and highly effective groups: there was very strong leadership in all departments. The Junior PCC met regularly to discuss the agenda of the official PCC – passing on resolutions as recommendations – and for Bible study, before breaking up to go into general youth activities.

In May of 1973 a new Lord Mayor of Manchester was elected, and asked me to be his chaplain. The automatic choice for many years as chaplain to a Church of England mayor of Manchester was Canon Eric Saxon, rector of St Ann's in the city. He was a former Head of Religious Broadcasting for the North of England from 1944 to 1951. I used to be impressed by his contributions to discussions on *The Third Programme* when he was a member of the formidable body of men known as 'The Brains Trust', even though I was an unbeliever and didn't know he was a priest. He was also chaplain to the Queen (1967 to 1984), rector of St Ann's Church and rural dean of the cathedral deanery, chaplain to the Manchester police, the health authority, the banks and offices, the department stores and much else. Not for nothing was he known as 'Mr Manchester'. During my early post-conversion years, I used to attend his Thursday midday office workers' services, drawn by his first-class but highly accessible sermons on topics chosen by the congregation week by week, and he was the greatest influence on my becoming an Anglican in December 1957. With his prominent background it was not surprising that he was stunned by my appointment, though he was mollified by the fact that I was the first ordinand of an eventual total of about twenty from his ministry at St Ann's.

The civic service was held in the cathedral on 27 May, and one took place later at St Richard's, on 3 June, and I preached in the cathedral on 9 September. I thoroughly enjoyed the council meetings, having worked in the city for a total of twenty-nine years (if we include the two and a half in Salford), and having for a long time been fascinated by the interface between theology and politics. A broadening of my experience also came in meeting the banquet guests, both national figures and royalty, and a highlight of the latter was a fourteen or fifteen minute conversation with the Prince of Wales when he came on 22 May 1974 to bestow upon the city a new charter.[12]

At about the same time, Bishop Ted Wickham asked me to become chairman of the Diocesan Home for Unmarried Mothers.[13] I declined, gracefully, I hope, on the grounds that I was shortly to leave the diocese for pastures rural. This brought from him a diatribe to the effect that I was 'throwing away all the respect I had built up in the diocese' (which surprised me) and 'prejudicing my future'. The truth was that I was worn out and in need of a complete change,[14] and Patrick Rodger, the diocesan bishop, agreed and offered me the parish of Sadberge in the diocese of Durham.[15] Joy told me when we had moved there that

---

[12] The original charter of 1838 having been concluded on 31 March 1974, under the new Local Government Act.

[13] Strange to think that such institutions existed as recently as 1973.

[14] Michael Hennell, my former Principal at St Aidan's College and by this time a canon residentiary of Manchester, discerned as much when we were walking together in Dovedale in March 1973. He promised to have words on my behalf with the bishops of Manchester and Derby.

[15] From the beginning of the diocese in 1847, the bishop of Manchester was patron of five parishes in each of three other dioceses: Carlisle, Durham and Lincoln. The historical reason for such a provision is inscrutable, but it was helpful for him, as a means for sending priests who had been burnt out in 'urban priority' parishes (about 50% of the dioceses of Manchester were of that classification), for four or five years, to recuperate before returning to the fray.

she had been close to a nervous breakdown, though, characteristically, she had not complained. Her distress was quite understandable, considering the unremitting stress and strain of constantly being at the mercy of waifs, strays, battered wives and beleaguered husbands while I was out 'working'.[16]

It had been a great privilege to serve in the front line of the battle, to have suffered in His service, and to have such vivid revelations of His love and His power in response to our prayers. During the course of the next period of our work we were to see many, further and different experiences of labouring in His vineyard.

---

[16] I ought to mention also the stress and strain on our children, Jillian and Jonathan. We had decided from the outset that we would not send them away to school, on the grounds that it would be a condemnation of the schools to which our parishioners, perforce, had to send their children. However, the constant subjection to a violent culture, one which despised excellence and high aims as 'posh', and therefore condemnable on 'class' grounds, had its deleterious effect on their life. On discovering this, when we had lived in the countryside for a while, we sent them, after much reluctance, and much prayer as to the fees involved, to private schools. It is an open question as to which answer we would come to if faced with the decision again.

3

Sadberge, County Durham, 1973–1978

> Nature never hurries; atom by atom, little by little, she achieves her work.[1]

Sadberge, a village between Darlington and Stockton, was the ancient seat of administration of part of what became a county based on Durham. To this day the county court is described as that of 'County Durham and Sadberge'. It boasted a history of Roman, Saxon (the church was putatively founded by St Wilfrid in the seventh century), Danish[2] and Norman rule. The field below the village school is listed as the site of a Roman settlement, and the building stone of the Norman church (replaced in the nineteenth century) was inscribed '1266'. The hill behind the Rectory is called Beacon Hill, and was one of the series of beacon hills northwards towards Scotland. It had a population of 697 in 1974 – varying from time to time with births and deaths – a figure ascertained while visiting every house in the parish. To be Rector of one country parish without a diocesan job as well, let alone several other parishes, was a privilege to be enjoyed for only a short time.

I had to re-gear my engine immediately. Seeing the farmers from my study window, working in their fields with a necessary but reverent regard for the seasons of nature – ploughing, sowing, waiting for the reaping, mowing and ploughing again – taught me very early that we custodians of human nature ought to learn to take one step at a time, and not try to force spiritual growth or

---

[1] Ralph Waldo Emerson, *Nature*, 1831.
[2] The name, I was given to understand while on holiday in Denmark in July 1973, is derived from the word *Sødbjerg* – 'flat-topped hill'.

intellectual ideas, no matter how brilliant or earth moving, onto people who had their own pace, their own Zen,[3] to be respected. One important thing that came from that observation was something I tried later to pass on to theological students: that on moving to any new parish it was wise not to make any changes for the first two and a half years. We all have an inbuilt non-acceptance of change, and even in these days of lay responsibility there can be some anxiety as to whether the latest incumbent is going to demolish their tradition, and a fear of what is to be newly introduced. Two years or so is also a good period in which to learn from them: what do they value, what are their greatest needs, what are their strengths? It was to me a massive sense of sitting down and listening to what God was saying in that place and at that time, to us, and through others. It was not time wasted; it was time well spent to get to know and to be known, no matter how impatient we may be to get things going in our own way, to try all our newest ideas and schemes. Of course, we may from time to time throw in suggestions for such things as study groups, outreach, stewardship or baptism instruction, and then leave them to germinate (or wither!) It is my experience that before the two and a half years have elapsed someone at a PCC meeting will say something like, 'What about that group you have mentioned? When is something going to happen?' That is usually a sign that one is beginning to be trusted, and can start moving things on. If the ideas are originally from God and not from our own enthusiasm, they will germinate. If they are not, they deserve not to.

Some methods of parish leadership, used by a number of colleagues, I never could be happy with. Most leaders fear the possible failure of a scheme or a plan, such as a mission or a stewardship campaign. This is a normal part of any kind of leadership which prays and thinks through the tension between prophetic initiation of policy on the one hand, and priestly sympathetic attention to where people are and what their capacity for immediate development may be on the other. To allay the

---

[3] I gained a lot at that time from reading *Zen and the Art of Motorcyde Maintenance* by Robert M Pirsig, which has stayed with me since.

anxiety of rejection, incumbents adopt different methods of securing success, or avoiding embarrassing setbacks to their leadership. Three methods stood out in my observation of others. One was to introduce the debate at a meeting of the Church council and then sit back and allow the various views to be expressed at length, without interruption, until either the subject, or the antagonists and protagonists, were completely exhausted – whichever came first. Sometimes, in Wythenshawe at any rate, according to a bemused curate of one parish, the meeting became divided into two sides, and the level of animosity would escalate to personal insult and physical conflict. The deadly thud of fist on face, with bellowed imprecations, would proceed for a while, during which the incumbent, faithful to his Christian pacifism, his pre-adopted plan or his non-plussedness, would sit silently and placidly, gazing at his order form. Eventually, exhaustion and hopelessness would set in, and in the silence the chairman would quietly put his motion to the meeting, whereupon it would be passed, *nem. con.* At about 11.20 p.m. Another leadership method was to visit every member of the PCC and urge them, on implicit pain of whatever sanction seemed most effective, to vote in favour of the motion when it was put. This was as equally effective, and in a much shorter space of time. Both of these methods, to my mind, involved the danger of leaving a faintly smouldering frustration and resentment, or at least dissatisfaction, in all but the most genial and submissive of church councils. The third method (though other gradations of the first two are possible) was the one I favoured, being neither a complete pacifist nor a dictator, though it was very simple, naive and, some would say, vaguely irresponsible. I made sure beforehand that everyone concerned with influencing or making the decision was fully informed about what was at issue. Then I would pray, not that God would vindicate my wishes nor my authority, no matter how right and godly I believed them to be, but that the Holy Spirit would move hearts and minds to obey His will for the issue. Whatever happened, I could then take no credit for the success of my own ideas, or have guilt, despondency or resentment if things went against me.

Sadberge parish church, County Durham. Photograph by Tom Elliot.

During my first week in Sadberge my two children, then aged thirteen and twelve, naturally graduated to making friends with the other young people in the village. One evening I took the opportunity to try to mingle with them myself at the bus shelter, only to find each time that they took off into the darkness, leaving my two on their own. I managed to track down one of the fugitives, and asked him why they all fled at the sight of me – something I had not experienced before. He said, 'Because you're the rector.' On further questioning it emerged that the rector, together with the head teacher and the village policeman, were seen as agents of authority, and therefore may well report to their parents any perceived bad behaviour. I assured him clearly that I was not in that social category, and would he spread the word that I would never report anything to their parents without clearing it first with them. The second occurrence with the local young people was that, towards the end of my time in Wythenshawe I wanted to arrange a residential conference somewhere for my Junior PCC, but had not succeeded in finding a suitable place. The vice chairman, Geoff Miller, suggested that as I was going to a rectory with a sizeable garden, they could go to Sadberge. And so it was arranged that under the guidance of St Richard's organist, Don Whalley, the youngsters would come north and camp out in the rectory grounds. The vicar of my new neighbouring parish, John Williams (who in addition to being a kind and compassionate priest, had a very interesting history[1]), was a great help in finding suitable speakers and enablers, and as a conference it went very well. But the presence of so many young people at the rectory, a circumstance previously unheard of,[2] excited considerable interest in the village. Cuttings from holly and hawthorn bushes found their way during the day into sleeping bags on the lawn, and sticks and stones hopped imper-

---

[1] He had been convinced of his vocation to ordination on a visit, during his National Service, to Belsen concentration camp. Although he was eighteen or so months younger than I, his father had met Abraham Lincoln and his wife's brother became, in 1979, the bishop of Manchester. John Williams went to be the bishop's officer for ministry in Lichfield diocese in 1983 until his retirement in 1996.

[2] My predecessor, for instance, had gone there to retire. He had been rector of Greenheys, Manchester: a most inappropriately named slum parish.

sonally over the walls, one of them hitting one of our girls on the head, drawing blood. She took it totally calmly – she was brought up in Wythenshawe after all. Things escalated, and on the third evening, during a group study, we became aware that the rectory was surrounded by marauding hordes, all curious to know what was going on. I went to the front door, and called for them to come in, but all I saw in the moonlight were retreating figures across the fields. I repeated my invitation, but someone said, in a stage whisper which was carried on the quiet crisp evening, 'Don't go in – it's a trap – he'll phone the police.' The youngsters I had previously encountered must have assured the others, however, for they all sheepishly, one by one, muddy boots and all, filtered into the house. Introductions all round, and Don Whalley went off to Stockton to supply us all with fish and chips. The third incident followed hard on that one. An empty articulated tanker lorry split in half on the bouncy road outside the rectory one afternoon, and the trailer demolished the fence opposite which bounded a field of pigs. The farmer's twenty-seven-year-old son and a goodly number of the village lads struggled to mend the fence and keep the pigs from getting away. By the time I returned home, the vehicles had been removed and the police were leaving the scene. While talking to the lads, I noticed that one police officer had stayed behind and was removing the traffic cones which had protected the wreckage. The farmer's son looked at me in alarm, for he and his helpers had nowhere near finished securing the fence. I went over to the policeman and pointed out that they still had to stand on the road to finish restoring the fence – wouldn't it be a good idea if he left the cones for a while? He happily agreed. The lads' faces were a picture when I walked back to them, 'You stuck up for us against the law!' they exclaimed. I tried to explain that it was a mutual agreement, not a conflict, but they were convinced that I had supported their side against authority, and after that I seemed to have the total confidence and cooperation of the young people in the village. This led to the formation of a youth club with a generous number of parents as helpers. A football team was started, with the striking colours of yellow shirts and green shorts – Norwich City for some reason, but they looked very smart. Joy was equally creative. It had been the tradition in the village that, during an interregnum, the produce from the fruit trees in the rectory orchard – plums, damsons, pears, apples – were fair game. The practice continued after our arrival (it had been a long interregnum while pastoral reorganisation was being considered), which put it in a slightly different moral and legal category. But instead of confronting them or their parents, she gathered baskets full of fruit over and above our own needs and took them round to the homes of all the likely lads, without mentioning the incursions at all. The families saw the subtlety, the 'raids' stopped immediately, and goodwill was established.

Not long into my time in the village (something like the two and a half years I have spoken of) things started to happen. A Methodist minister missionary from West Africa visited Darlington on furlough, and persuaded his 'home' congregation that the charismatic experience ('baptism in the Holy Spirit') was the will of God for our generation. This led to the formation of a charismatic prayer group, and I was asked if I would be one of the leaders, together with two Methodist lay preachers and a Roman Catholic monk (I don't know why – I hadn't mentioned baptism in the Spirit to anyone east of the Pennines, though Joy worked in Darlington as a health visitor and may have spoken so to a Methodist colleague). The group met monthly in Darlington, and attendances averaged over ninety, more than half of whom were Methodists, with a large contingent of Roman Catholics (including several nuns), some Salvation Army members in full uniform and, until the arrival of a charismatic new incumbent at St John's Church adjacent to the railway station, just two Anglicans. These meetings were a source of great encouragement and hope. The charismatic movement in the 1960s and early 1970s was seen by many to herald a large-scale renewal movement in the Church; but repression of it in the Roman Church, and suspicion generated largely by emotionalism or outright perversion in the other denominations, seemed to dissipate its effect. If it had been God's attempt to rejuvenate His people, it ran very sadly into the sand, though its effect on new church music was widespread, and still endures.

About halfway into our time in Sadberge I had a delegation at the door of the rectory: half a dozen or so village lads complaining of a shortage of things to do in the school holidays. Could I suggest something? I said I would give some thought to it, and suggested that they get together and return with some suggestions for a concert in the village hall. It wasn't long before they came back with a proposal for an evening's 'television programme' – sitcoms, sketches, advertisements, news broadcasts. After some discussion they went away again, and turned up after a day or two with some imaginative and hilarious scripts. I made some adjustments and drafted a suggested running order, but the final lines, action and direction were decided by them. There was much scepticism from villagers that their local lads and lassies would be able to rise to such an ambitious undertaking, but great was their astonishment and pleasure at what the youngsters proved themselves capable of. We had far more material and volunteers for participation than we were able to use; they were magnificent, and the evening was a resounding success.

I have never been quite certain about refusing offers or invitations to move, or take on extra responsibilities. We always had a rule that we would never actively seek to move away to another parish, but rather await 'direction' or 'guidance' from wherever it came; and not to refuse an offer of fresh responsibility, in case it came from God. On the broadly 'structural' scale – that is, of main responsibility – this policy served us well. We could have opted out of Salford when the living conditions got on top of us. But who wants to start off a ministry by switching to somewhere else when the going gets rough and experience a ministry of two year stints for thirty years? The people of God in Salford suffered the same hardships as we did – what sort of servant of them would we have proved to be? The custom of founding new parishes in new housing areas was for a senior curacy of some two and a half years, then moving to a living, leaving an incumbent-grade priest to take it on to a consecrated church, and parish status. We were left in Wythenshawe through the whole process, complete with makeshift vicarage,[3] for ten years. The five-year break in the country was just right for reflection and regrouping in order to tackle what came to be our 'main work' in Durham. The offers I had after three and a half years in Sadberge – to return to the Manchester diocese to a parish in Bolton, or move to a housing estate in a Durham mining town – did not ring true at the time, especially as my excellent church warden, Ronald Richardson of Sadberge Hall,[4] a man of great spiritual discipline and ethical business sense, had been given only six months to live.

Another new venture was my involvement in the pastoral reorganisation of the Darlington deanery. The archdeacon of Auckland instituted a deanery commission in the autumn of 1975 to investigate the number, placing of and need for each of the church buildings in the town, in the light of late twentieth-century changes in population and social conditions. Like so many towns in England which were transformed by the Industrial Revolution and the coming of the railway, Darlington had created an optimistic number of parishes, and with the decline of heavy industry and retrenchment of the railway system, the picture had changed radically.[5] I was asked to chair the commission, presumably because I was one of the few incumbents without multiple responsibilities, but I enjoyed it very much. It went into great detail in its social and ecclesiastical analysis, and it attracted some very gifted people in the deanery. We went away for a few days as a body in 1976 to the York Diocesan Retreat House, to have an intensive 'bash' at the formation of our report. One of my most vivid memories of that conference was, at the end, accepting the offer of a lift home (I was without wheels at the time) from Scilla

---

[3] With Gordon Thorne, we designed modifications to meet Church commissioners' regulations for parsonage houses, and during the interregnum these were effected.

[4] Former home of the Pease family, of Quaker and Stockton and Darlington Railway fame.

[5] Until as late as 1966, it was said that fourteen to fifteen percent of Darlington's male working population was employed on the railway. This made for a close-knit and stable (if introverted) society, which was shattered by the closing of North Road locomotive works in that year.

Riley Lord.[6] Scilla was a larger-than-life spinster, lay chairman of the diocesan synod and General Synod member, a delight to be with at any time, except – by repute – in her car: she drove an open-top racing car, giving a fair imitation of James Hunt or Nicki Lauda in doing so. With what was left of my hair sticking out horizontally behind, I was whisked through North Yorkshire in a most exhilarating fashion, pleased that I hadn't a long scarf like Isadora Duncan, arriving home breathless and much earlier than had been thought possible.

In September 1975 I was invited to become a part of the voluntary staff of the newly formed independent local radio station, Radio Tees. I offered myself as a potential writer of scripts for the 'God Squad', but was immediately co-opted onto the microphone, to front the Problems Phone-in Programme, because someone decided I had an 'avuncular, chocolate-sounding voice'. I was advised to adopt a pseudonym for the purpose, in order to prevent a plethora of phone calls at home (I was not doing it as a clergyman), so I became 'John Altrincham' for an hour each week. The programme produced problems from the general public of a very wide-ranging nature, from the little girl whose cat refused to come down from a tree, to the lad in matrimonial difficulties in Gateshead (I advised him to go and see his vicar, to which he protested, 'You can't talk to them!' He did so, however, and rang back a fortnight later to say that all was working out well). There was also an old couple besieged by some antisocial behaviour at their corner council house in Middlesbrough. The town council were most helpful when I wrote to them – with permission from the programme controller – about the problem, and rehoused them elsewhere. After some months on that rather demanding and on-the-spot exercise, I crossed to the news reading and features presentation. This involved interviewing people who were either spokespersons for a particular subject in the religious news (Islam was one of them), or notable Christian visitors to the area.

---

[6] She was the daughter of Captain Sidney Riley Lord of the Grenadier Guards, one-time sheriff of County Durham. She had clearly inherited a spirit of confidence and elan.

Under the last heading came a Pentecostal Evangelist from New Zealand, who painted pictures as he preached, and then gave them away afterwards. His was a healing ministry, and he was to follow his agenda in Stockton with a campaign in Darlington. By November 1977, Joy's diabetes had caused her to lose her sight except for partially in one eye – saved thus far by laser treatment – and I asked her if she wanted to attend one of his meetings. At first she demurred, not willing to get involved in some emotional or charlatan road show, but later she agreed to attend and assess for herself the nature of the spirituality on offer. The gentle and unemotional presentation of the gospel, the coming forward of people from the previous evening's service – placing their crutches and spectacles on the dais – convinced her, and at the 'appeal' she went forward to receive the laying on of hands. When her turn came, the evangelist recoiled suddenly, saying, 'My, the Lord gets to you, doesn't He?' Nothing seemed to result from this, so we went again the following evening. The same thing happened, and he was genuinely puzzled that she had not been healed, but declared that her sight would not deteriorate any further from her present state. That proved to be true for the remaining seventeen and a half years of her life.

Why she was not healed, having the great faith she had, was a disappointment, but it seems that from time to time we have to learn that God is not at our command. This was demonstrated to the worldwide charismatic movement a few years later when, despite an enormous wave of earnest prayer around the globe, Canon David Watson – one of the movement's leaders, with a well-known healing ministry, and to whose guidance and inspiration hundreds of people owed their faith – died of cancer at the age of fifty-one.[7] One is reminded of Voltaire's experience when taxing the archbishop of Paris with all the problems of Christian belief. Being met with firm faith, however, he eventually said, 'It seems to me that your God cannot fail!' The archbishop replied, 'Precisely.' Joy pursued the rest of her ministry and her life within her physical limitations, which was a source of great admiration and inspiration for those around her.

---

[7] His death caused much bewilderment and heart-searching; but God is not our servant – we are His (Isaiah 57:1–2).

In October 1976 the government's job-creation programme swam into our ken. This measure engaged unemployed and unskilled young people in locally sponsored schemes, overseen by experienced and qualified supervisors. Materials for the schemes were supplied by the benefiting body, and the government paid the wages and expenses of the staff. The qualification for the projects was that they would benefit public bodies and charities, and thus their communities. I was quite enthused about the whole concept, and started with a plan for substantial repairs and rebuilding on Sadberge church. I was able to organise, over the next eight or nine years, about seventeen schemes in my own parishes and those of others in the diocese.

Early in 1978 I received an invitation from the dean and chapter of Durham to move to St Cuthbert's, Durham. We had enjoyed our recuperation time in a country village; our theology of ministry, tempered by a realisation of the different pace of life in town and country, and by having a much smaller reservoir of resources, had registered for the Kingdom in several respects. We knew it was time to go.[8] As we considered the offer, the omens were mixed. The congregations at St Cuthbert's were small, but the people of the parish contributed handsomely to church funds. This hinted at enormous possibilities for growth – and so it proved.

The roof of the church building was extremely water-friendly, welcoming it in at every opportunity; and the vicarage, a huge end-of-terrace four-storey Victorian edifice with twenty rooms and three 'little rooms', suffered from the same generosity all over the place, and was in a seriously run-down condition. The arrangement whereby the church wardens could 'test' the wisdom of the patron with a visit to or from the prospective incumbent was just coming in; which was fair enough, except that the new rubric was interpreted very enthusiastically, and half the PCC visited Sadberge Rectory one evening. I supposed that with several county hall officers and university lecturers they were

---

[8] Part way through my five years there, a church warden said to me, 'No man under fifty worth his salt would be content to stay long in a parish like this!' I was not yet forty-five years old.

cautious to see what kind of man they were going to get this time, and a thoroughgoing 'interview' took place. After that meeting, a large army of volunteers in the parish formed itself into a first-class cleaning and decorating team for the vicarage. The diocesan secretary – who lived in the parish, though worshipping elsewhere – commented on the near impossibility of such a thing happening, on the grounds that none of them did even their own cleaning and decorating – a deduction which proved profoundly wrong. We moved in three months later than originally planned[9] because of all these preparations, and the induction took place in December 1978, just before the snows came and stayed for the first three months of 1979. Walking (it was impossible to get the car out) in January up the Front Street of Framwellgate Moor (part of the old A1) where the daughter church was situated, the temperature, with the wind-chill factor, was reported as -27 °C. We had arrived in the true North.

---

[9] Though I was kept abreast of the news in the parish, and in fact visited a church warden, Ralph Powney, and the treasurer (later a reader and then a non-stipendiary curate), Bryan Middlebrook – who were both ill – before the official induction.

4

Durham City, 1978–1994

> To speak of God at all in human language is to verge always on nonsense. He is mysterious and his ways are mysterious. In the end, for all our devotions, theologising, and earnest intentions, we have to acknowledge, with the great Thomas Aquinas, that our strivings for understanding have been as straw, in the face of the glory that is to come.

It was clear before we arrived at St Cuthbert's that the parish was suffering from some serious problems. One of these was that the main service of the day on three Sundays of the month, Mattins, was attended by only six (superb) old ladies (the other Sunday had a family Eucharist, led by the associate priest, a lecturer at St John's College,[1] which was attended by some thirty or forty persons). But the leaking church roof was a more immediate concern. Any substantial rainfall gave rise not to a steady drip but a rush of water from the junction of the tower and the nave roof just over the main entrance, and an early service of Evensong was marked by the explosion of light bulbs and serious aquatic ingress in the apse. Efforts had been made to raise the money necessary for repairs, but unsuccessfully, and the problem was getting more expensive to solve by the week.

I told the parochial church council that if God wanted St Cuthbert's to remain open[2] then He would provide the where-

---

[1] Peter James Hedderwick Adam, a most un-Australian Aussie (non-cricketer, non-rugby player, but a first-rate organist, French horn player and canoeist), who became a valued colleague, and a companion fell-walker. He was to return to Oz and be successively the archdeacon of Melbourne, chaplain to Melbourne University and principal of Ridley College, Victoria, in that proud country.

[2] The patrons, the dean and chapter, had considered closing it – there were six other churches in the city and it was by far the least well attended. Investigation

withal to repair it; if He did not, then we need not worry about it. So we started to hold prayer meetings on a Saturday evening, and the money soon came in. The meetings continued, at the wish of the leading participants, as a service of compline for years afterwards. The parish turned out to be of the 'Midas' category,[3] in the sense that as soon as an initiative was prayerfully launched, it took off of its own volition, and the leadership had to run to keep up with its development. As the vicarage was in a poor condition, too, the diocese told us at first to look around for a suitable alternative parsonage house, but we failed to find one. The church people thereupon formed a working party, as mentioned, under the leadership of the church warden and county engineer John Petrie, consisting of all sorts and conditions, who laboured hard to turn it into a house which would prove both suitable to live in and, in time, for large-scale rural deanery gatherings.[4]

Joy's ministry among women flourished (by this time she had lost nearly all her sight, though later it improved slightly). Developing from her experience in Wythenshawe, her study groups, organisation of retreats and, latterly, a meditation and prayer group, together with leadership of a mother and toddler group, gave new dimensions, new perspectives and spiritual growth to many. As the rural dean's wife she also ran a clergy wives' group, which was found very helpful by those who attended it regularly.

One of my first delights after arriving in Durham was to be invited to lecture to the students at Cranmer Hall, St John's College, on the philosophical and theological work of G W F Hegel, having once expressed my opinion at an in-service training session in Darlington as to how much more inspiring Hegel was

---

showed, however, that its finances were in healthy shape, and that it was, according to one member of the chapter, 'a church which people paid to stay away from'.

[3] As distinct from the 'old car' type which keeps moving so long as the leadership is pushing hard, but stops when the effort ceases.

[4] After ten years, serious roof problems at the vicarage proved to be too great for any reasonable further expenditure, and it was replaced by a newly-built house near the Land Registry. But it had served well.

St Cuthbert's church, Durham. The county hall is in the background.

Durham Cathedral drawn by Warnsley and engraved by Humble: 'spiritual splendour solidified'
(Lucinda Lambton)

than Kant. This led to further engagements with the ordination students and being admitted to membership of the St John's College Senior Common Room. Another pleasure was attending, in Durham Town Hall, the 'Medieval Disputation on Christianity and Politics'.[1] It was good to witness a debate where positions were put forward without interruption and responded to directly, point by point. The subject was one in which I had long been interested, having sought in political philosophy a practical interpretation of reality during my time as an atheist. From 1979 to 1984 I was a lecturer on the North-East Ordination Course (NEOC), dealing with Applied Theology – the urging of students to continue their theological enlightenment after ordination and to think through explicitly the theology which was implicit in all they did in their parishes. I always bore in mind the pre-ordination admonition of the principal of St Aidan's to 'always have a big book on the go' – that is, to keep abreast of scholarly theology. Academic theology and the philosophy of religion have developed greatly since the 1960s. The earnest parish priest will endeavour, so much as lies within him or her, to keep abreast of the discussion of problems pertaining to his assumptions regarding the nature of God and our conception of Him. This present memoir, while not ignoring this continuing discussion, is concerned with a supportive theology and an effective faith-interpretation of that theology. At the coalface the miner was not concerned with the geological formation of the substance, but with an efficient and safe way of making it serve ordinary people. For a couple of years on the NEOC, this involved being counted as on the staff of Newcastle University, for the ordinands of the Newcastle diocese – an experience which was to be offered to me again twelve years later, when I was asked to be a lecturer on John Henry Newman on the Applied Theology Masters degree course.[2]

I was appointed as rural dean of Durham in 1980, in succession to Gordon Roe, who had left St Oswald's parish to become the bishop of Huntingdon. There were twenty-one parish units in the

---

[1] 13 November 1979.
[2] Though I was not able to accept it, to my regret, because by then I lived so far away.

deanery, one of which had a Methodist place of worship as the parish church, jointly manned as an area of ecumenical experiment. There were twenty-eight priests and curates, plus seventeen or so 'sector ministers' (university chaplains, lecturers, doctoral students from all over the Anglican communion, chaplains for social responsibility, the hospitals, and arts and recreation), and about – at any given time – twenty-eight retired priests. Membership of the deanery synod had to be worked out carefully according to Church House Rules, in order that these constituents should be fairly represented without swamping the meetings with clergy. Synod debates were of a high calibre because of their presence,[3] but the chairman had to exercise much wisdom to ensure that the representatives of the pit villages in the deanery were encouraged to make their contributions without inhibition or feeling overwhelmed by the clergy or the city and university lay representatives.

Rural dean's parties for clergy and spouses were held once a year, spread over two evenings because accommodating seventy-odd clergy and the spouses (about 130 all told, though not everyone came every time) was not practicable at one go. Nobody paid to attend, and nothing was claimed on expenses: I thought the whole exercise was worthwhile, but did not want it to be a strain on the deanery budget. The diocesan bishop was always invited as a way of meeting all those clergy and wives in a relaxed way. The dean and cathedral clergy were not, as they had their own chapter, but the four bishops in the deanery were.[4] One of the many joys of these gatherings was, in 1985, to introduce the new bishop of Durham, David Jenkins, to a predecessor, Michael Ramsey, for the first time.

There were three notably lively churches in the city – St Oswald's, with a fine musical tradition, dating back at least to the incumbency, between 1862 and 1875, of John Bacchus

---

[3] No fewer than nine priests from the deanery of that period were made bishops – four from the university and five from the parishes.
[4] These were Michael Ramsey and Joan, retired from Canterbury; John Moorman and Mary, retired from Ripon; the Suffragan (Jarrow); and Harry Moore and Betty, retired general secretary of the CMS.

Dykes[5]; St Margaret's, a Catholic-tradition charismatic church under Stephen Davis; and St Nicholas's Evangelical charismatic congregation with George Carey (who was, for a while, the deanery chapter clerk). These last two congregations contributed a significantly large proportion of the diocesan income. My first deanery Eucharist was held in the cathedral on 11 June 1981. I shall always remember the occasion because of half a sentence in my sermon which mentioned that one of the encumbrances of the job of a parish priest was modern theologians and their constant undermining of the traditional assumptions about the faith. I returned home after the service, rather tired, and had switched on the television to watch the news when a sudden chill at the heart came at the realisation that the new dean, Peter Baelz, had just come[6] from Oxford where he was the very model of a modern theologian. Sure enough, the next morning's post (such was the GPO's promptitude in those days) brought a letter from him, asking me to expound and explain. This I did, in the terms of my struggles in the 1960s to justify the traditional doctrines against the tide of the age, and the way I had found such an assumption very effective at 'street level'.

His was the far finer intellect in this exchange, but in a very courteous way he replied that he quite saw my point, and what could he do about it? I suggested two things: one was to accept invitations to preach in the parish churches, to present his views to the 'ordinary parishioner', which he subsequently did, with spectacular impressiveness. The other was to meet the deanery clergy and address us on the relationship between theological speculation and modernisation, on the one hand, and the need to expound and deepen understanding of the traditional gospel of healing and salvation to people where they were, on the other. This he also did, at a rural deanery chapter meeting held at the cathedral deanery on 9 February 1982. A good discussion took place, one which he and I took up and developed each time we met afterwards.

---

[5] 1823–1876, composer of many hymn tunes, services and anthems.
[6] The dean, the bishop of Jarrow, and the rural dean had been newly appointed in 1980, which gave us common conversational ground, though their responsibilities were far greater than mine, of course.

When, in 1984, the 'Durham Affair' exploded, at least one deanery had discussed the issues which it raised, and was ready to cope with the arguments, one way or the other. On 25 May[7] of that year, in response to suggestions from various parties, I called a meeting of the clergy at St Bede's College, inviting the cathedral chapter as well, to discuss modern theology and pastoral care in the light of the problems raised by the new bishop-elect's forthright utterances on basic doctrines such as the Virgin Birth and the Resurrection. A very lively debate ensued, and when the time came for me to sum it up, the cathedral clergy, including the dean and the Canon Theologian Stephen Sykes, left to avoid the possibility of being caught up in a vote (they were going to have their own debate and vote before long, in the national legal framework). Sure enough, at the end, three or four clergy proposed a vote, in the hope that sufficient support would be gained for their opposition to David Jenkins's appointment. I resisted such a conclusion to our meeting, on the grounds that no enduring good would have been served by a dichotomy of loyalty among us, and that the meeting had taken place as part of our continuing interest in the conservative/liberal problem. When the press began bombarding the cathedral and diocesan staff for comments on 'the affair', it seemed that they all with one accord began to excuse themselves (understandably so – they were all going to have to continue working closely with people on all sides of the dispute, whatever the outcome). Thus it was that I found myself the recipient of phone calls from several quarters, most interestingly from seven or eight newspapers, for my opinion on what was taking place. I was able to say that the whole issue was part of a continuing discussion we had been having for three or four years, and was therefore not as earth-shattering as they assumed. I soon learned to temper my vocabulary to the level of understanding displayed by the questions put to me. Clifford Longley (then of *The Times*) was well up with the theology involved, as was the *Yorkshire Post*,[8] but some of the others were looking for secular concepts on which to hang a headline or a sound bite.

---

[7] St Bede's Day.
[8] David Jenkins was in Leeds at the time.

I wrote a booklet on the Durham Affair,[9] in which I tried to interpret the progress of liberalism – some healthy, some negative and deadening – from *Essays and Reviews* in the nineteenth century to *Honest to God* and its sequels in the twentieth. It was, I think, only partially successful. My main argument, and the one I worked on in the face of questions from parishioners, was the policy adopted by the staff at my theological college, St Aidan's. With each intake of new ordinands, they made the evangelical students face the problems of Biblical interpretation thrown up by textual criticism. The liberal students were challenged to question the shortcomings of sociology, psychology and the sufficiency of human reason; and the catholic ones to question seriously their ecclesiology. The process of reducing to pulp all their Sunday School theology made them start afresh to build up on a sound basis a theology which would stand up to the stress and strain and unforeseen hazards of ministry – a ministry which rested on Christ and not on derivative doctrines and a jejune understanding of them.[10] It was a sound policy, the evidence for which was clear in the subsequent ministry of students of St Aidan's: there is a characteristic soundness and faithfulness in them, an echo of the Holy Spirit's loving faithfulness, in the ministry of those nurtured in that tradition.

A generation on, I am not sure that Bishop David was about that at all. He was advocating, I think, a thoroughly 'modernist' approach to faith and its contents: what can be faithfully adhered to in the face of the philosophy department's scepticism, and the conviction that the traditional assumptions of 2,000 years were unreal today. But his approach produced some seminal discussions: I was stopped on the street by retired miners wanting to

---

[9] *Dear Jonathan: Letters to an Ordinand on the Durham Affair*, Chester-le-Street, Casdec Ltd [Educational Publishers], 1985. The Jonathan in question was my son, who at that time had been thinking of ordination, and had received a very courteous and welcoming letter in response to his application for entry to a theological degree from the Revd Canon David Jenkins, Professor at Leeds University.

[10] It sounds like the regime of a spiritual boot camp, but in those days of acceptance of fierce discipline and willing and humble submission, it was almost entirely successful.

know what I thought about what he was saying. I always asked first what *they* believed. As in Alexandria in the early years of the Church, when the dockers were discussing finer points of theology, the working men and women of Durham were talking about them, too. One of my choir women, a nurse, came to the vicarage one morning: could she have a word with me? She came straight to the point – she had always had trouble with the Virgin Birth, and now she could say so to my face, because the bishop had, as it were, authorised her doubts. After an hour's discussion, she went away believing in the Virgin Birth, but added that she hadn't dared to tell me before because my faith seemed so rock solid. This incident taught me that an apparently 'rock-solid faith' could be something of a barrier to effective ministry, rather than invariably an asset, and was duly chastened.

I think, for what my assessment is worth, that Bishop David was torn between an evangelical position of believing the traditional faith, but being embarrassed as a deep-thinking theologian by the closed-mindedness of some of the proponents of that position, and lashing out against them. That he was, in his interior belief, open to God in all his traditional unexpectedness and glorious untrammelled vastness, I am convinced. I remember the first induction he conducted in the deanery, in the old mining parish of Pittington.[11] His sermon followed well-composed but rather dry and academic lines until about a third of the way through, when he suddenly went off like a spiritual rocket, and illuminated the way in which the needs of that particular parish could be met, carrying the good people there with him.

After the service, he asked me, 'Was that all right?' I thanked him, saying that the Holy Spirit seemed to take him over part way into his address. He replied, 'Did you notice? I thought so too!'

If humility is the hallmark of a Christian and a good bishop, then David qualified handsomely.

Humility was also a characteristic of his predecessor, John Habgood, a hard act to follow in the fullest meaning of that

---

[11] The church at Pittington is believed to have been a 'dry-run' for the architecture of Durham Cathedral.

term.[12] The picture painted of him in the press was that of a cool, detached figure, highly rational (as befitted a former research scientist), but lacking in warmth of feeling. This was a grave injustice and very far from the truth. There were many instances of how compassionate he was. One of our deanery clergy, facing a sudden crisis in his family life, rang him up and was invited to go to Auckland Castle immediately, without regard for the Episcopal diary. My friend was received warmly and with sympathy and was helped enormously, and I am sure that similar occasions could have been reported from other deaneries in the diocese. I myself experienced a truly humble attitude from both John Habgood and David Jenkins; an account of such incidents could be read, totally inappropriately, as implying some merit on my part, so they cannot be detailed – but happen they did.

Peter Baelz was, as I have indicated, another man of stature.[13] I warmed to him immediately for his humanity and openness. After our early contretemps we had a running discussion, resumed where we had left off as we met from time to time. On one such occasion he said, 'I have come to the conclusion that even if the faith be totally untrue, following the Christian path was a good way of having spent one's life on earth.' I was a bit stunned by such total reductionism, but on reflection thought it was a version of the German philosopher Hans Vaihinger's 'as if' doctrine.[14] This was that mankind needed 'pragmatic fictions' in order to deal with reality. By this, to live 'as if' the Christian proclamation were true, even without believing its texts to be historically or philosophically valid, is a form of faith. To be unselfish, self-giving, seeking the common good above all, aiming for the heights in every activity of which human beings are capable, is a

---

[12] One of his senior officers said to me once that his admiration of John Habgood 'stopped short just this side of idolatry'. Many of the rural deans of his time felt exactly the same.

[13] In more than one sense: for a brief period, before the retirement of the then bishop of Jarrow (Alexander Hamilton, 1965–1980), the diocesan, the suffragan, the dean and the archdeacon of Durham were all between 6'2" and 6'4" tall, giving a strong impression that height was a qualification for eminence.

[14] Hans Vaihinger, 1852–1933.

'good' way to live.[15] I also wondered if being faithful in the face of such thoroughgoing intellectual doubt was not a greater exercise of faith than that of people like myself, who had received an undeniable and existential experience of God which overwhelmed any intellectual misgivings. In those words, Peter seems to have been musing on the view expressed in the Doctrine Commission's report of 1976, 'Christian Believing': 'Faith is an adventure in which a Christian is staking everything on the belief that this way of using our one and only life will in the end be validated not only as the best for human condition but as most truly in accord with ultimate reality'.[16]

It ought to be added that by no means were all twentieth-century theologians of the critical or reductionist camp. Austin Farrer, for example, is still praised by fellow theologians for making historical Christianity intelligible in terms that were both traditional and contemporary, both orthodox and original; a theology well thought out, but grounded in experience.

The new bishop of Jarrow, Michael Ball,[17] was another with whom I enjoyed discussion of these questions, and who, with university staff, contributed to our debates prior to the Durham Affair of 1984. We were blessed in having so many able men and women around at the same time, especially Ruth Etchells, principal of St John's College, who was very helpful, among other ways, in a conference I mounted entitled 'A Theology of the Workplace', and Ann Loades of the Theology department. Someone else who made a deep impression was Michael Vasey, of the staff of Cranmer Hall. His spirituality was almost tangible, and although he died a sadly early death, he has left an indelible mark on us, and on the Church's liturgy.

It may be helpful to clarify, at this point, the ways in which the liberal/conservative debate is most inflective of pastoral ministry.

---

[15] Cf. 'To live for the other is the best way of living as a human being' – Pope John Paul II; and some words of the composer Arnold Schoenberg: 'If God did not exist, the accumulated faith of generations would summon him into being.'

[16] Extract taken from p.3. The report was rejected by the Church, presumably because it went too far in the direction of radicalism and reductionism.

[17] 1980–1990, later bishop of Truro.

It seems to me that the main categories are: revelation (the nature and authority of Biblical inspiration); the 'laws of nature'; doctrine (for example the Resurrection, the Ascension, miracles); postmodernism; the Incarnation; the zeitgeist; and fundamentalism.

Revelation

My teenage rejection of the Christian faith, on the grounds that religion was for women and children, not red-blooded men, was given intellectual foundation on a reading, among other books, of Tom Paine's *The Age of Reason*, published in 1795. His merciless dissection of the New Testament, according to the application of Enlightenment logic and pragmatic common sense, was a comprehensive demolition of its authority, authorship and credibility. He anticipated the Biblical theories of the nineteenth-century German scholars, Strauss and Bauer, Renan's *Quest for the Historical Jesus*, the observations of Nietzsche and Herbert Spencer, and of Rudolph Bultmann's attempts to salvage a Christian gospel free of myth and the supernatural. Having come to faith through such a welter of scepticism, I came to regard as folly the chopping away at the details of the text on the basis of certain scholarly hypotheses which were not at all entailed by inescapable facts, until only a circumscribed, not a wholehearted, commitment to the Christ of tradition remained ('the death of a thousand qualifications', as someone has said). The Gospels claim to report the words and works of God incarnate. If they were only 'symbolically' what they recorded explicitly and materially, if Jesus is removed from historical scrutiny so that we feel safe and secure from philosophical criticism, if He is worshipped as a vague mystical 'best of history's good people', it appears to me that we have condemned Him to a still greater implausibility and powerlessness in everyday life. Because of my experiences under God from 1954 onwards, I am totally convinced of an unsceptical view of Scripture and Tradition.[18] I do not believe that God

---

[18] By this, I do not mean 'unscholarly', simply that much 'Biblical criticism' starts from assumptions which are not made necessary in the evidence produced for those assumptions. I warm to the summary of his magisterial work on *Christian Tradition* by Jaroslav Jan Pelikan, the great historical theologian (1923–2006):

would set up a Church and authoritative scriptures which would deceive or mystify us. Chipping away piecemeal at such foundations with a scholarly hammer and chisel does not impress me at all, having a faith forged out of the ruins of the carpet-bombing of Tom Paine.

The Laws of Nature[19]

A common liberal argument to miracles is that *God cannot transgress the laws of nature when He deals with man and the creation.* The laws of nature are in fact the rational organisation of our observations of the world around and within us. They enable us to rely upon architectural and engineering operations, our prediction of the consequences of our decisions, our practical living, and that our mathematics and physics hold good for space as well as on earth. But it is a step of faith to argue from there that God is imprisoned by these limits of our understanding of the universe and all that is in it. The advance of scientific knowledge shows us that at any given time we do not know all there is to know. This means that we cannot live firmly in the belief that we do; or that our corpus of well-established knowledge is sacrosanct for ever. It is also a step of faith to believe that science will, in the course of time, lead us to know everything. Advances in science are a joy and a fascination; but they affirm a coherence of nature which speaks of a mind behind its creation which is reflected by our own minds, by which we discern its rationality. They are certainly not a progressive revelation of the non-existence of a creator. Neither is the Creator-God limited by our comprehension and understanding of His creation. If He is so limited, is He not a god made in our own image? Such a god is not the God revealed in scripture and the life of the Church.

John Habgood adopts the scientist-theologian's view on this subject, saying that just as we have minds of our own, and are not predetermined by our brain-science, so God has a mind of His own, and is not totally and mechanistically determined by the

---

'Tradition is the living faith of the dead. Traditionalism is the dead faith of the living.'

[19] As distinct from 'natural law', which is a common instinctive sense of natural morality.

laws of nature that we rely on for our everyday calculations and activities.

Doctrines

The criticism of such miracles as the Incarnation, Ascension and Resurrection of Christ by mid-twentieth-century theologians on the grounds of logic and reason have begun to look like fundamentalism; the fundamentalism of a scientific view based on what is now an outmoded theory of matter. The visionary viewpoint of theologian-scientists like Teilhard de Chardin and his modern equivalents has begun to look far more cogent and balanced, as doing justice to the whole range of human value and endeavour, than the simplistic reductionisms of old. The Incarnation of the Second Person of the Holy Trinity, marking the unity of divinity and humanity, of spirit and matter, foreshowed the final transfiguration of the two aspects of reality – faith and reason. The new heaven and the new earth, towards which the whole creation is moving and the Church seeks to journey, will be the consummation of both spheres.

Scepticism is not, of course, an invention of the last four hundred years. The Sadducees did not believe in the resurrection of the dead, the survival of the soul or the existence of angels. Thomas the Apostle refused to believe in Jesus' Resurrection until he had proof which convinced him. The disciples were not gullible simpletons; they all doubted the women who said they had seen the risen Jesus. Even while praying for the release of St Peter from prison,[20] they dismissed as nonsense the maid's message that Peter was standing outside the door waiting to come in: they were actually praying to God for it to happen, but humanly speaking it was impossible, so they did not believe her.

It used to be asserted that although the Gospels were not a true representation of what actually happened, they remained 'symbolically' true. The story could be spiritualised to make it independent of history and of disproof, so that theologians might carry on with their church life as if nothing had changed. But of course, if the events described did not actually happen, the Gospel

---

[20] Acts 12:5–15

accounts couldn't symbolise anything. In more recent times, there has been a move to jettison the doctrine of original sin, presumably because it is 'nicer', or more consonant with 'human rights', to assume that everybody is born without a bias towards misbehaviour, simply with neutral inclinations. I always thought it were better to retain the theory which best explained human perversity, rather than abandon it in favour of an intellectual idealism which was conjectural. Marxism went wholeheartedly for the eighteenth-century assumption that people are born neutral but are distorted by bad economic and social conditions, bad education, bad parenting: if we put all these things right, then people will not be bad. But in a world where one of the most cultured and highly intelligent of nations can be led to set out to massacre all races classed as *Untermenschen*; where groups of eleven and twelve-year-olds in our own civilized country can terrorise a child to death and then broadcast the incident on the internet; where rape, murder and disfigurement of young children by gangs of young men coarsen our news items each week; and where leaders of governments across the world can demonstrate vividly that 'absolute power corrupts absolutely', the abandonment of original sin seems to be flying in the face of fact. Perhaps theologians who are giving way to the pressure to do so, especially those in the Evangelical camp, have suffered at the hands of the Calvinist version of original sin as a condition of 'total depravity', 'entire corruption', from which only the 'elect' – those predestined by God to deliverance from utter and eternal damnation by his prior choice – can escape. The utter pessimism of this position leads inevitably to fatalism, and it may be this extreme version of original sin, which portrays God as an unjust judge rather than a loving and forgiving father, which they are seeking to rid themselves of.

Postmodernism

Since 1989 the world of ideas has moved on swiftly. Marxism was finally shown to be as false a scientific substitute for Jewish and

Christian millenarianism as all the others,[21] and philosophers have reacted by condemning all grand narratives as untenable. According to postmodernist thought, no matter how we interpret history and its foundation documents, the idea of a past that should determine our present is illusory. The notion of a theory that has an inception, an application in the real world, and a denouement at some time in the future was no longer to be considered a valid or useful interpretation of reality, whether philosophical, political or religious. It is an affirmation of the illusion of a *search for the truth to be applied to life*. It is *my truth is as good as your truth* in all walks of life and endeavour. *Authority is discredited and oppressive, and the concepts of goodness, worthiness and excellence, as opposed to bad, are elitist. We all make our truth as we go along, unhampered by predetermined principles or codes of morality.* But a society in which every person or government leader makes his or her own value-system is a world heading for nihilism, chaos, total mistrust and an absence of law and order.[22]

Such a radical attack on what has always been held to be at the rationally objective foundation of intelligent discourse, and of personal morals and political ethics, cannot be supported in Christian teaching as giving any sort of information about a way of living for Christ. If grand narratives of interpretation are out, then the Church and all its baggage is out, and no attempt to accommodate the Bible to such modern ways of thinking will come anywhere near convincing the secular man on the Clapham commuter train. The liberal agenda of adjusting the Faith to the latest philosophical threat has had its branch sawn from under it.

---

[21] Its downfall was clearly foreseeable in the summer of 1974, as I said to Natasha, a highly intelligent and educated Party member, whom we met on a visit to the Soviet Union. The contemporary Five-Year Economic Plan had included, for the first time, consumer items such as handbags and fashion shoes and gloves. The shop assistants had been found putting items on one side for themselves (paying for them, but making sure the goods didn't sell out before they could buy them). Natasha was horrified that the third generation of post-revolution youth could exhibit such self-seeking behaviour. The Enlightenment doctrine that human beings were born ethically neutral, and what had been called original sin was really a product of bad economic/social conditions, was a falsehood at the heart of Communism. The gradual realisation of this error was the seed of the collapse of the whole edifice.

[22] Unless imposed arbitrarily by force.

It seems that we are faced with the alternative of loyalty to the Faith as it has come down to us (while admitting that its divine inspiration has been mediated by men, but not so as to distort the message)[23] on the one hand; and on the other, homogenising the gospel and modern thinking to the point of becoming indistinguishable.

I suppose none of us relishes the thought of appearing to live in a bygone age, of being subject to a world view of 2,000 years ago; of respecting as divine the cosmological and theological speculations and interpretations of a comparatively primitive Middle Eastern tribe. But as Michael Ramsey used to tell his ordinands, 'however contemporary we may try to be, our orthodoxy rests upon an old, old, story.' If the life of Jesus, in the way it is reported, was actually a revelation of the eternal Creator-God, then it is valid for all time; and the appeals to a loving Father who knows not only every Sudanese peasant and Oxford professor but every hair on his or her head, ought to be valid in terms of perceptible response, as it was in Jesus' earthly life. If such a God made provision for the transmission over generations of a collection of sacred writings in order to preserve the accounts of contemporary witnesses of the nature of the unique God-Man, then it stands in a very special category for ever. Theology needs 'modernising' in the sense that revelation is progressive: the scriptures are an endless source of fresh inspiration to preachers and hearers, and new approaches to their relationship to life are constantly being produced by advances in knowledge of all kinds. Few people outside the kinkiest other-worldly literalisms can deny that our understanding of the complexities and wonders of the planets and stars is increasing enormously, as is our knowledge of the DNA structure, of carbon dating procedures, of computer and medical miniaturisation and all the other intricacies of electronics in the service of humankind. A theology which does not take into account such discoveries and inventions will not make much impact

---

[23] Fundamentalism, in the sense of literalism, is faith in the letter, not the spirit. It is a reversion to legalism (2 Corinthians 3:6; cf. Romans 2:29 and 7:6). Rationalism, even when based on inspired texts, is still human reason, not the Holy Spirit. The words are pointers to the Lord, but our faith is in Him, not in the words instead of Him. Our loyalty to the scriptures is based on the belief that they have been given to us by Him to lead us to, and to educate us in, Him and His nature. In this, they are 'fundamentally true'.

on people whose lives are influenced by them. Understanding the nature of a God who is not merely the God of religion (in fact, 'religion', as a construct of the human desire for God, can obscure God), but the God of everything, cannot fail to involve all aspects of human understanding. It constantly seeks to hammer out appropriate and practical ways of speaking about the Divine – ways which, by their nature, must be metaphysical and allegorical. It is a complex and sensitive process, based as it is on a personal relationship, and not at all the simplistic exercise to which it is so often reduced. But all such understanding and interpretation make sense only on the basis of a full acceptance of the revelation in scripture. At base, the whole enterprise rests on a child/father relationship which is immediate and straightforward in its trust and faith.

I was heartened by some words of Archbishop Robert Runcie in a sermon he preached at the Church of St Mary the Virgin, Oxford, to a Bible study course which I attended in July 1985. He said,

> I am for the Bible when it is treated with reverence and understanding, when we recognise its right and power to address us and are open to receive whatever it may say. I am against the Bible when it is treated as a resource or store from which to draw sanction [...] for any opinion we may hold, or anything we may wish to say.

The Bible stands in judgement of us, not we of it; through the ages, men and women of all nationalities have found it to be revelatory of the things of God and the things of their own nature. He continued:

> The root meaning of 'understanding' is a posture of 'waiting upon', of being attentive, reverent and eager to receive whatever may be disclosed or given [...] It does not suggest a posture of scrutinizing, analysing or weighing up, nor one of grasping, controlling or mastering.

The tradition, from the nineteenth century, of treating the Bible as one would treat a human text, has produced much which has been helpful to understanding. It has helped to see where 'inspiration' has been tempered by 'inspired imagination' – for instance, in the Creation chapters of the Book of Genesis; slight discrepancies between ancient manuscripts of the New Testament show an emendatory hand (for example, in I John 5:7). But such minor changes do not alter the theological doctrines: the Bible is consistent with itself when 'understood'.

The view of the philosopher and historian Paul Ricoeur (1913–2005), his 'second naivety', I found helpful when I came across it: the idea that after studying the text, and trying to grasp the scholarship which has been brought to bear upon it, it is still possible to come to it with the childlikeness which Jesus commended to case-hardened adults, and listen to the Father speaking to the depths of our being. Ricoeur's doctrine referred originally to the proposition that myth and symbol, as a figurative interpretation of reality, were part of human consciousness before the ability to interpret rationally the world of which we find ourselves part.[24] He argued that the loss of the original belief, which spoke of meaning and hope in a world apparently indifferent to both, could be recovered not by reverting to a pre-critical attachment to myths and symbols, but by an interpretative gesture of a 'second naivety'. The concept of naivety of any kind is hardly one to commend to modern sophisticated man, but 'scepticism' can be the first step in a corrosive and destructive process: sceptic, cynic, agnostic (about all knowledge), atheist, nihilist, unassailable pessimist and depressive. And their succession can take place unnoticed in oneself. Scepticism has been called the father of unbelief, and the mother of a total rejection of the whole tissue.

The Zeitgeist

> We must keep up with the spirit of the age.[25]

> The Christian knows that his function is to divinise the world in Jesus Christ.[26]

---

[24] He was dealing primarily with the account of the origin of evil in Genesis.
[25] Lord Rothermere, joint founder of the *Daily Mail* in 1934, as he supported Hitler, Nazism and Oswald Mosley's Blackshirts.
[26] Teilhard de Chardin, *Le Milieu Divin*, (Collins: [Fontana] 1957) p.72.

Today's main question, rather than that of the first, eighteenth or twentieth centuries, is whether the zeitgeist, the spirit of the age, is the same thing as the *Heilige Geist*, the Holy Spirit; whether the voice of the people is the voice of God; whether there is any meaningful distinction, in this twenty-first century, between 'secular' and 'sacred'; whether whatever developments take place are of God, and if not, how do we distinguish between those that are, and those which are not? Has the Church a duty to move completely with the times and modify its doctrines and ethics to accord with what people as a whole are actually doing and thinking (or even, in our own time, to deny that 'God' is part of reality in any sense), or has it still an age-old commission to warn, to rebuke, to specify what is 'good' and what is 'bad'?

The great German writer Jean Paul Friedrich Richter (1763–1825)[27] wrote that 'good education will always be counter-cultural, because every culture is idolatrous. It is held captive by the "Spirit of the Age", rather than by the Spirit of Eternity.' Since his day, many queries have been put to the terms 'education', 'idolatry', 'this age', 'the Spirit of Eternity'; but the Christian Church has seen itself traditionally as counter-cultural on Richter's terms. If it is by its nature counter-cultural – standing where necessary for something over and against what the majority of people actually believe and do, and against trends in society – it is necessarily going to be in some respect 'other' than the society in which it is located. If the 'something other' is not defined or definable, in terms other than what it stands against, has not the yeast lost its function?[28] This question of the spirit of the age is, it seems to me, one of the problems thrown up by the system of the philosopher and theologian G W F Hegel. If the rational is the real, and the Incarnation of God in Christ is the revelation of God in the form of matter, then 'reality', in all its forms, is an epiphany of the Creator Himself, and whatever happens is 'real' and therefore part of the rationality of the Creator. This raises the

---

[27] Who put forward the concept of 'reverence for life' fifty years before Albert Schweitzer, holding that 'visible things are symbolic of the invisible'.

[28] '"Catholicity" is that which offers something distinctive to the world without being captured by it.' – J S Habgood, *Confessions of a Conservative Liberal* (Society for the Propagation of Christian Knowledge, 1988) p.90.

questions of 'sin' and occurrences such as natural disasters (earthquakes, tsunamis, typhoons and so on), which have to be looked upon as the continuing birth pangs of matter, initiated at the Big Bang; and the humanly-caused catastrophes as part of the divine self-limitation which allows human beings freewill to accommodate wickedness and the rebellion of evil against the love of God. I suppose that the duty of the Church is to help to distinguish between a valid movement of ideas into legislative action, and an invalid one (individual and corporate sin) which endangers the development of goodness and godliness in society and ordinary people. But the validity of cultural and intellectual trends and developments is a notoriously difficult field – witness the case of Galileo.

Referring to a well-known problem with Hegel's system does not inflect my view that it does away effectively with the duality of matter and spirit.[29] He attempted to reconcile the spiritual and the material, essence and existence, the ideal and the real, arguing that these opposites were brought together once and for all in the Incarnation.[30] These dualities are behind most dismissals of 'miracles' and the 'interference' of God in the laws of nature. It does away also with the duality implicit in certain theories of the Atonement: in particular, the separation of the Father and the Son which speaks of Jesus placating the wrath of an outraged Father, rather than the Son's revealing the Father's taking responsibility for all the sins and horrors of the world, and revealing His great love for it.[31] God is the Lord of all reality, for all that happens, and is responsible for everything (cf. Isaiah 45:5 and 7, KJV). The consecration of matter in the coming in human flesh of the Second Person of the Trinity has far-reaching consequences for our faith. In this context we would be wise not to use the word 'secular' ('of the world') in a wholly pejorative sense, that is, in distinction from the spiritual; or as a way of thinking and acting as

---

[29] The most masterly exposition of Hegel's theology, to my mind, is that of Hans Küng, in *The Incarnation of God* (T & T Clark Ltd, 1987).
[30] Thus his exhortation to use the day's newspaper as a source of subject matter for prayer – a concept now thoroughly part of our intercessory lives.
[31] 'God was in Christ, reconciling the world to Himself' (2 Corinthians 5:19).

if the spiritual does not exist. Positively, the Spirit of God, as well as inspiring the people of God, was the agent of the creation of the universe.[32] After all, 'The earth is the Lord's and the fullness thereof, the round world and all that is therein' (Psalm 24:1). We must claim the world for Christ, but that is not the same as saying, 'We must claim the world for the Church.' That would be to narrow down the words 'secular' and 'Church' far too much. We must be prepared to rejoice at the creativity and benefit to human amenity of many developments in areas which seem to belong solely to the world of politics, sociology and architecture; for instance, in the rejuvenation of the city centres of Salford and Manchester in the last twenty years. Similarly, in the world of the arts – literature (novels and poetry), painting and the performing arts which have their own reflections of truth, and can produce for us glimpses of the Holy, the sacred, the metaphysical (meaning that which is truly other than the bare logical and scientific, as revealing the inner nature of human creativity).[33] Much modern art, by denying the validity of attempting to portray the deeper truths of life, simply reproduces life in its brutal superficiality, and by doing so denies the craving of the reader/viewer/listener for something 'beyond and behind' it all, which human beings instinctively know exists. The greatest of art throughout history reaches out for the qualities which express the divine qualities – beauty, transcendent truth, true peace and true prosperity in human affairs – and does not merely echo the base and destructive instincts inherent in human nature. In an age of marvellous advances in nearly all forms of scientific endeavour – and we do rejoice in its wonders – we still remain the same human beings as we were. We may draw parallels from the discoveries and their application, and some may claim that such ideas and benefits should have caused a similar evolution in human nature. But they have not. We have still an enduring feeling of unease that scientific advancement leaves untouched the deepest yearnings and questionings about 'Why?' and 'What for?' and 'What should

---

[32] Genesis 1:2 and Acts 2

[33] 'A theologian who does not love art, poetry, music and nature can be dangerous. Blindness and deafness toward the beautiful are not incidental; they are necessarily reflected in his theology' (Joseph Ratzinger).

we do?' As Austin Farrer argued, in his doctrine of 'Double Agency', God's initiative is in everything and everywhere. This is intuitively behind all our yearnings for stability and happiness. Our response to God determines whether we are open to His initiatives, and thus to further responses in faith and grace. It is a dialectical process, not one of blind static rules, such as those offered us by science, or denied us by dead-end philosophies or religions. This dialectical process of being led by, and being developed, by God is offered to us in each and every department of human endeavour. Christians are still called to be 'holy'. They are called to a holiness which is far removed from sabbatical sanctimoniousness, and much closer to affirming people where they are, and pointing them in the direction of the fullness of a spiritual life: a holiness which illuminates from within a life which is lived in this world.

The Transfiguration of Jesus is an event which I have always found inspiring, because it speaks to us, through the witness of Peter, James and John, of their friend being transfigured – illuminated in the flesh by the glory of the Father, as the light of the world. This was in the midst of everyday earthly responses and worldly concerns and ways of thinking: Peter simply wanted to stay there, close to heaven, prolonging the joy. But when they returned to the foot of the mountain they found the other disciples in a theological mess over how to deal with a demon-possessed boy.[34] When Jesus had healed him, the disciples asked Him why they had been unsuccessful, and He told them it was because they had so little faith. Later, His promise to His followers was that they would do greater things than He did if they trusted Him.[35]

Theology has been described recently in these words: 'The governing intent of theistic discourse is to refer to a transcendent God, an extra-mundane source of a providential order in the world.'[36] This is a good concise description as long as 'extra-mundane' is not meant exclusively. The God of the Incarnation

---

[34] Matthew 17:1–20
[35] John 14:12–14
[36] Peter Byrne in *God and Realism,* Ashgate Publishing, 2003, p.155.

and the Crucifixion of the Second Person of the Trinity is not completely extra-mundane, but involved inseparably in the world and its affairs. Deism is an ever-ready safety net for those who have a great problem with traditional Christian beliefs, landing them however with a more insoluble one: a God who is required to interfere in a self-regulating universe in response to prayers, and the concomitant questions of omnipotence and capriciousness and the inherent contradictions of His interference. I hope I have made it clear that I hold firmly to the practical nature of God's relationship with ordinary people who put their whole trust and confidence in Him.

On a different theological tack, in 1984 Billy Graham returned to the UK with 'Mission England'. One of his venues was Roker Park, Sunderland, then the home of Sunderland FC, and I immediately joined the rehearsals of the Durham portion of the Mission Choir, led by Cliff Barrow. The whole event was a great experience, and once I had been identified as a priest I was appointed as a team leader for the counsellors at the rallies. I left the ranks of the choir each evening at the appropriate point, and stood beneath the preacher's podium to receive enquirers as they came forward from the stands. There was hardly an evening when the 'sea fret' didn't invade the ground, and the platform team and the choir could not see a soul through it.[37] But it was an inspiring experience on the first evening to stand on the pitch, following the preacher's 'call', to see, emerging from the fog, a large group of bikers in their leather metal-studded jackets, dyed hair, jeans and bovver boots, accompanied by their girlfriends. Soon the whole pitch was full with people of all ages coming forward with open hearts and minds to hear the message that Jesus loved them; that He had paid the price for a new start in life, and the opening of the path to love and salvation. I had encouraged the people of St Cuthbert's and St Aidan's to go to the meetings, and many of them did so. One of St Aidan's people, who was the Chief County Fire Officer, sat in the stands as people went forward, taking in the spectacle, when he suddenly thought *It's wrong just to*

---

[37] Dr Graham announced that it was the first time he had ever preached in a cap (and probably in a muffler and overcoat, too).

sit here, and went down to the pitch. He found himself standing next to one of his firefighters, who said, with astonishment, 'What are you doing here, sir?'

'The same as you, my lad,' replied the Chief.

As with all the great rallies of that era, 'enquirers' were referred to the local churches, but differences of theological approach, and the difficulty of integrating new people in established congregations, caused several to fail to establish themselves as members of Christ. But many heart-warming things were reported, and the bread is never cast unfruitfully upon the waters. Each year after that I was asked by the 'March for Jesus' organisers in Durham to set off the march round the city streets with a short service and prayers, from the bandstand in Wharton Park overlooking the city.

A happy relationship, after a cold and frosty beginning, was forged during the 1980s with the Roman Catholics at St Godric's. There was only one other place of worship other than our own two in the parish – the Methodist Chapel at Framwellgate Moor, to whose people we were very close. But just over the parish boundary, near the railway station, was St Godric's[38] Gothic-style church, on a commanding mound overlooking the city centre. At my meeting with the rural dean of Durham just before I took up the appointment at St Cuthbert's, I asked him about ecumenical relations, in particular with the Roman Catholics.

'Forget it', he said. 'Several have tried with Father Rice and failed.'

I paid a courtesy call upon the said gentleman however, and sure enough, on the doorstep, after I had announced who I was and the purpose of my visit, he said, 'Yes? What do you want?'

I explained that it was a courtesy visit, and so with great reluc-

---

[38] Godric was a very interesting and unusual saint. Born near King's Lynn, he lived as a pedlar until he went to sea and became a prosperous trader. One chronicler describes him as a pirate, and certainly in his early life his business methods were dishonest and his lifestyle disorderly. But in middle age (he lived to be over 100 years old, 1065 to 1170) he became a hermit to make amends, and lived for his last sixty years at Finchale, three miles down the River Wear from Durham. He is regarded as the earliest known lyric poet in English, and his hymn tunes make him the author of the earliest known settings of English words.

tance he asked me in. We sat there for some minutes, his wariness and lack of interest in me quite obvious, until I mentioned the priest at St Anne's, Darlington, in whose bailiwick Sadberge had been. His face relaxed a little; it emerged that the two of them had been curates in Stockton together years before, and that the other man's Irishness had been as humorous and charming to Frank Rice as it had to me. We parted on warmer terms than we had met, but they could not have been described as friendly.

We met again when we dedicated a new Cooperative Funeral Service Chapel of Rest at Framwellgate Moor, and as we were leaving afterwards, he suddenly came back and said, 'We must get together sometime.'

During that period there was spate of arson attacks on churches – two in our deanery, one in Bishopwearmouth and a couple on Tyneside – and one day St Godric's was hit. The church interior was burnt out, and three or four churches in the city offered Father Frank and his flock the use of their building for worship. He accepted our offer, mainly because of our car-parking space, and they worshipped at St Cuthbert's for more than two years, boxing and coxing on a Sunday morning, and sharing non-Eucharistic services as often as we could.

When St Godric's had been restored, 50% of the congregation declared that they would have preferred to stay at St Cuthbert's, but the diocese of Hexham and Newcastle had naturally set in motion from the outset the rebuilding programme, and it was a sad day when they departed. We shared together the first Easter ceremonies in the restored church, a notable feature of which was that the Exultet was sung by our (very musical) female student-on-placement: a permission which surprised everyone on both sides of the denominational and gender divide. Relationships had been changed for ever, though. Frank said later that prior to all these events he had not regarded Anglicans as human beings, let alone Christians. When he retired, he gave me a copy of a monograph he had written on St Godric, and we kept in touch until he died.

As I have mentioned, working with young people became an important part of my ministry. I was blest in Salford with a Boys' Brigade company, and in Wythenshawe with a Church Lads'

Brigade (a spin-off unit from the mother church), and then a Church Girls' Brigade company was formed. There was also at St Richard's a Cub Scout pack, and a first-rate Girl Guide company which produced a succession of district commissioners. We had nearly 250 youngsters and excellent leaders in these uniformed organisations. People who would not have seen themselves suitable for leadership were asked to accept responsibility in these bodies, and proved to be ideal in the roles. A characteristic of the life of the CLB at St Richard's was to be beaten most years into second place in national sports competitions by a company from 'up North'. It was my privileged surprise to find when I moved to Durham City that this unit of rival excellence was based at St Aidan's Framwellgate Moor, in my new parish. During my time in Wythenshawe I had attended the annual camp, held at Humberstone, Cleethorpes, and after 1978 I went each year to the North-east camp with my new company, as an assistant chaplain, as well as attending officers' training conferences at Cookham Manor, on the Thames in Berkshire (Stanley Spencer country). I was able to take a minor leadership part in all the camp activities, except swimming and canoeing (being a non-swimmer made those pursuits rather inadvisable – though I went sailing a couple of times), and rock climbing, to which I was not attracted initially, but experience in attempting to climb all the mountains in England and Wales (i.e. over 2,000 ft)[39] and a proportion of the Scottish Munros (mountains over 3,000 ft), led me to take instruction, from 1990 onwards, in rock face manoeuvring and abseiling. When I retired in November 1994 I was granted the rank of regimental chaplain, with the bishops of Durham, Jarrow and Newcastle, so that I could continue to attend camp. Alan Smithson, the bishop of Jarrow and later the national chaplain to the CLB, shared a talent for watercolours with Keith Wynne, the colonel of the Durham/Newcastle regiment, and initiated classes in watercolouring for the young people, among the varied camp activities. Some of the most unlikely lads from the pit villages came to enjoy that activity, after a very cautious start, and produced some creditable work.

---

[39] The completion of which became the second of my three 'retirement projects'.

I have an enduring admiration for the commitment of such youth leaders. They were totally unpaid, gave up part of their annual holiday each year as well as evenings each week, were open about their personal faith and standards of life in their service of young people. The continuing attraction of an organisation with strict discipline, highly developed rules and a code of healthy activity, strange in the post-1970s culture, was testified to by the number of youngsters from run-down mining communities, who otherwise were at the mercy of a culture of low, or at least amorphous, standards in everything. The uniforms, and the corporateness inculcated by army-type drill, and based on a church milieu of worship and service to others – derided though these things were in a postmodern era – seemed to give them a self-respect and a point of reference beyond their feelings of dissatisfaction, worthlessness and bewildered rudderlessness.

The Junior Parochial Church Council, a concept for which I always waited until I had been about nine or ten years in a parish before drawing together,[40] developed as a post-confirmation group. As mentioned above, membership was by election, voted on by all members of youth organisations, plus other young people who attended church. The agenda for the meetings was in two parts: the first comprised a run-through of the agenda of the next meeting of the statutory PCC, to give the young people a view of what their church (and it *was* their church – they were not 'tomorrow's church') was most immediately concerned about. Where important decisions were to be made by the legal Church Council, the issues involved were discussed, and a vote taken. The result of the vote was then delivered by the members who were also on the adult PCC, and the adults were always magnificent in taking it into account in their own decisions. On at least one occasion (concerning liturgy) the Juniors' decision was backed unanimously. The second part of the meeting would sometimes be a Bible study, sometimes a speaker – especially in Durham, where there was a plethora of sector ministers, most with interesting backgrounds and media awareness. Every parish priest always hopes that confirmation candidates will continue to

---

[40] Thus two parishes in all.

develop in faith and vocation, and I have been greatly blessed with my share of such encouragement, some of which has come from following it up with experience in a Junior PCC.

★

> Faith [...] is not simply the intellectual adherence to Christian dogma [...] It means the practical conviction that the universe, between the hands of the Creator, still continues to be the clay in which he shapes innumerable possibilities according to his will.[41]

St Cuthbert's was a parish full of industrial chaplaincy and sector ministry opportunities for its incumbent. In its boundaries were the following institutions: the county hall; the police HQ and northern training centre; Durham Hospital; the county psychiatric hospital; the ambulance HQ; the HQ of the county fire brigade; the Land Registry (latterly two); a central office of the National Savings movement; two working farms (latterly one); the Northumbria Water Board HQ; an office of the Central Electricity Generating Board (latterly closed); the East Coast Main Line railway station; and a large college of further education and teacher training, with two campuses. I was not the 'official' chaplain to all these establishments – the health authority operations had their own, as did the county hall and (eventually) the police – but I was formally appointed to New College and to the fire brigade. The fire brigade chaplaincy involved a yearly conference of chaplains at the National College at Moreton in Marsh in Gloucestershire. This was always highly enjoyable and inspirational, and I developed a great respect for firefighters. The discussions I had on visits to the stations in the county often had a greater theological content than some ecclesiastical meetings. This list represented a very large (and largely optional!) workload, considering my responsibility for a two-church parish and a rural deanery, and it is fairly obvious that not all of it could have been done with any depth of thoroughness. But 'something' was better than 'nothing'. The needs of students and staff at the college, and the men of the fire brigade always took pastoral

---

[41] Pierre Teilhard de Chardin, *Le Milieu Divin*, p.134.

priority at a given time. New College had a service in the cathedral every two years in the 1980s, until a change of policy under a new principal, and the fortieth anniversary of the founding of the Fire and Rescue Service in the county (in April 1988) also saw the cathedral as host to our celebration.

In 1984 the diocese launched a 'prayer pilgrimage': every parish had a day allotted to it when it would pray for the corporate life of the diocese and its own mission statement. The symbol chosen to be passed on to the next parish was not the best in everyone's judgement. In an attempt to avoid obvious 'churchiness' and navel-gazing (we assumed), it was to be a miner's lamp. This was taken to be a symbol of the life of County Durham, though the half of the county which had never known coalmining and whose industrial symbols were more likely to be connected with agriculture, railways or heavy engineering were thereby alienated or, at any rate, left feeling like Queen Victoria. The intention of the scheme was that at the end of the 'pilgrimage' the symbol was to be passed to the Durham deanery, and I was asked to list a sequence of parishes, culminating with St Oswald's and the cathedral. There were several spare days before the cathedral was due to receive it. Accordingly, as we were being exhorted to think in terms of the secular life of the diocese, and St Cuthbert's mission statement included all the above-mentioned non-churchy establishments, I included some of the larger of these civic institutions as places of lodging the lamp for twenty-four hours, and therefore inclusion in the prayer cycle, in the days allotted to St Cuthbert's, with their enthusiastic agreement.

Unfortunately, the day on which the county hall was scheduled to hand the pilgrimage symbol over to the police HQ (before passing it to the hospital and from there to St Cuthbert's), followed the worst day of violence on the strike picket lines, in clashes between the miners and the police. As many of the county councillors were ex-miners, the action of handing over a miner's lamp to the police was not an attractive thought, but more a gesture of surrender. The meeting at which the outrage at this proposal was expressed called in the Coal Board chaplain, who explained that I was responsible for the arrangement, and asked the bishop to intervene. David Jenkins immediately took charge of the symbol (which, had it been a crucifix in the first place, as many had argued, could have been a symbol of peace rather than of division, though of course no one could have foreseen the concatenation of events), and phoned me to say what had transpired, and would I go and pour oil on some very troubled waters.

On my way over the five hundred yards or so to the county hall, I decided I would not be on the defensive and point out my labour-movement qualifications (I had been a member of a trade union while most of them were still at school – and in some cases before that). Instead, I asked the Holy Spirit to go before me in those and all my doings, and further me with His continual help. The room was palpably seething when I entered, as the villain of the piece. But the Spirit was also present, and we parted on friendly terms, a relationship of warm goodwill which persisted in all my subsequent dealings with the county councillors involved.

I felt very honoured to be chosen, with Joy, as the representative parish priest of the diocese to be presented, with the two bishops and the rector of Ushaw College and Seminary, to the Queen Mother when she visited the cathedral in 1987, on the 1,300th anniversary of the death of St. Cuthbert.[42] For three brief days in November 1992 I was in charge of services at the cathedral. The occasion was the General Synod vote on whether females should be ordained as priests, and not one of the resident cathedral staff wanted to miss that historic decision. I have, since my very first visit during my ministry selection conference for ordination in January 1958, been immensely fond of Durham Cathedral. It has an atmosphere of numinousness, peace and faith which few other cathedrals have. My conviction is that the reason lies in the fact that it is the only cathedral in Britain which has the bodies of two saints buried in it. In fact, only Westminster Abbey has even one, presumably because not even Henry VIII was in the business of throwing out a royal predecessor, despite the fact that St Edward the Confessor was a 'pilgrimaged' saint. The reason why his

---

[42] St Cuthbert was born in 634, became the bishop of Hexham in 684, and the bishop of Lindisfarne in 685. He died on 20 March 687, his body was removed from Lindisfarne in 875 and buried at Durham Cathedral in 999.

minions did not dispose of the bones of St Cuthbert from his feretory was that they found not his bones but his body, looking as if he were asleep. In their panic, and rush back for further orders, they overlooked St Bede at the west end altogether. On 4 May 1993, I was to be present on the railway station at the naming of Class 91 locomotive 91002, 'Durham Cathedral', by Dean John Arnold; though, as he wore only a lounge suit, I was incongruously dressed in choir habit, which was the traditional garb on such occasions.

My attitude to the ordination of women was, from the beginning, not one of ecstatic enthusiasm. When I was the editor, from 1959 to 1961, of the college magazine at theological college, the principal commended me to write to Professor Geoffrey W H Lampe for an article on the subject. I was new to the Faith, and quite ill-equipped to cope with such recondite ideas, but of course the article, graciously written and duly received, was published. Over the years that followed, the debate began to be refined in my mind until all the relevant issues were clear; but I was not coping at all with my old unease from the days when I had rejected the Church and the Faith on the grounds that it was for women and children, and not grown men; and while I had overcome such a jejune position on my conversion, I could not overlook entirely that, on the evidence of numbers, it could still be so argued by an outsider. My fear was that the further feminisation of the people of God would be a curious development, given that God seemed to be the creator equally of males as well as females. The Rev Geoffrey Studdert-Kennedy's book is still a fascinating and very helpful examination of the creative tension between what we would, in our day, call the battle between Mars and Venus – in our minds, in our homes and in society – and its reconciliation in Christ. I was sitting next to David Jenkins one day at a luncheon function of some kind, when he said to me, 'Why are you against women priests? You are an intelligent person in all other respects.'

I replied in one word, 'Prejudice.'

He responded that he'd never before heard that given as a reason, and I explained that I could dress it up in all sorts of arguments – Biblical, historical, sociological, but that was the honest answer. I tried to explain the background, and how the relative absence of men, by and large, was a source of theological dismay to me. Not long after the first women had been ordained, a conference was held at St George's, Windsor,[43] to discuss how the Church was going to adapt to the widening of the culture of ministry which this development would cause. Unexpectedly, Bishop David sent me as his representative to the conference. In the study group I chaired, I brought up my particular concern, and our scribe reported it faithfully to the plenary session in the words, 'While accepting women in the ordained ministry, we are concerned as to why the Christian Church, the Community of the Redeemed, was disproportionately representative of the human race. Where was the place in it for Testosterone Man?' Some debate on the point ensued, with enthusiastic support from most of the women present, but several of the men suddenly found the carpet minutely interesting. I am still exercised by the question, though it must be said that (a) not all congregations are deficient in men: St Aidan's Framwellgate Moor, Durham, for example, consistently had more males in the congregation;[44] and (b) I have always been supportive of women who were convinced of God's calling to ordination, it being no duty of mine to put my prejudices in God's way. God had called my Church to ordain women, and I was not going to deny them that divine privilege.

I went on a three-month sabbatical study leave at St Deiniol's Library, Hawarden, in September 1989, during which (with support of the PCC, my curate, Bryan Middlebrook, Bishop David Jenkins, and guidance from Canon Professor Dan Hardy), I studied the relationship between politics and theology – the practical ordering of human society with regard to theological principles, from Old Testament times to the present day. This

---

[43] The day after the serious fire at the castle.

[44] Just as the congregations in places like Wythenshawe were 'working class' by any reasonable definition, so there were church wardens and other officers who earned their living by manual work. It should be said, also, that it is not solely a Church of England problem. I have been to Roman Catholic services in villages in Eire and Germany where the congregation of seventy-odd included only two or three men. I know several women who would have a ready answer to the question, but not one with which I could happily concur!

was most generously paid for by Bishop David. He even offered to pay for Joy to go with me, but she declined on the grounds that I would benefit more from being undistracted, though I popped home every ten or so days. It resulted in a 100,000-word essay, which I very much enjoyed writing. The subject of how the ordering of human society related practically to the principles of theology had been close to my heart since my conversion in 1954, and the study formed the basis for the first of my three post-retirement projects – a Master's in Applied Theology, with a dissertation on German politics since 1871.

On 1 April 1991, our daughter Jillian was married in St Cuthbert's church. She insisted that for once I put my family persona before that of parish priest, so I agreed to give her away rather than perform the ceremony. The bishop of Durham kindly agreed to do the honours, having met her while she was a lay chaplain at London University some years previously, and the priest of her fiancé's Roman Catholic family, Father Joe, assisted. As the bride and groom, his brother Sean Doran[45] who was best man, and the bridesmaids, were all dressed in special suits and dresses made specifically for the occasion, I too decided to do the same, and wore a clerical frock coat. This I hired from a theatrical outfitters in Newcastle, who told me that it had last been hired for the filming of the television series *All Gas and Gaiters*. As a rural dean, I could legitimately have worn gaiters too, but did not, and left it to family and friends to judge the appropriateness or otherwise of the programme's title.

★

> What would the world be, once bereft,
> Of wet and of wildness? Let them be left,
> O let them be left, wildness and wet;
> Long live the weeds and the wilderness yet.[46]

---

[45] In later years he was the artistic director of the English National Opera Company.
[46] Gerard Manley Hopkins, from the poem 'Inversnaid', fourth stanza.

In May 1990 I completed, with three others, the Three Mountains in 24 Hours walk, scaling the highest mountains in each of Scotland, England and Wales: Ben Nevis (4,406 ft), Scafell Pike (3,210 ft) and Snowdon (3,560 ft). This was a sponsored exercise in aid of the Church Urban Fund, and the four of us were blessed with beautiful weather throughout (except for a brief flurry of snow in the sun as we came down Ben Nevis) and with (the *sine qua non* of that exercise) excellent car drivers. I felt so well at the end that it occurred to me that with a helicopter it should be possible to do the highest mountains in Scotland, England, Wales *and* Ireland in just twenty-four hours. I wrote to RAF Boulmer, in Northumberland, for a possible itinerary, and received a very helpful and courteous reply, detailing a timetable which made the suggestion perfectly feasible with a helicopter. My response, by return of post, was to ask if the RAF could help us, perhaps as a joint exercise with the Irish army (Carrauntoohil, at 3,414 ft, being in County Kerry). But the international complications were too intricate, and they offered Slieve Donard, in the Mountains of Mourne, instead. Whatever one's political views, Slieve Donard, at 2,796 ft, is not the highest mountain in Ireland, so the proposal fell through.[47]

Approaches to Barratt's Housing, who had until recently been helicoptering the actor Patrick Allen into their new housing projects, and to Sir Richard Branson, were not fruitful either, though Sir Richard, in a personal letter, did say it was a great idea and would like to do it with us if ever it came off. My final exercise in heavy mountaineering was to sign up, in February 1993, for a mountaineering course and a traverse of the whole of the Cuillin Ridge on the Isle of Skye, to take place in late September of that year, a few days before my sixty-fourth birthday in October. What I thought was incipient flu came upon me soon after, and I thought I would have recovered entirely by the time it came to depart, but it emerged that it was not flu but the onset of a slowing down due to the ageing process. There were many enjoyable and exciting experiences during the four days of the

---

[47] Years later, this became one of the few regrets in my life. Northern Ireland is part of the United Kingdom, and it would have made history to have done the 'Four Mountains in 24 Hours' under that definition.

course – two days' instruction, and two days doing the ridge – but I was much the slowest member of the party, and it was with some relief to me and the next-slowest person when, after camping overnight in a cave near the summit of the ridge, we awoke to find the whole range covered in two or three inches of snow. One of our guides had recently returned from Everest, and he said that no one would venture on the Cuillin Ridge in that condition. So the expedition was cut short, and we made our way down the Great Stone Chute of Sgurr Alasdair to Glen Brittle, and I have never done the western half of the Ridge. But we had climbed the 'Inaccessible Pinnacle', which Sir Hugh Munro himself never accomplished, and the two highest peaks on the Cuillins – Sgurr Alasdair and Sgurr Thearlaich – and negotiated Collie's Ledge. This adventure marked a turning point in my expectations of myself, which applied in the work, too: I began to be unable to keep up the traditional 'three-session day',[48] and experienced significant weariness for the first time. I resigned the chaplaincy to New College (a new principal had not, for several years, seen the same need for a chaplain as had his predecessor), and retired from being the rural dean. Joy's health was becoming a factor, also. Her diabetes had given rise, in addition to her retinopathy, to increasingly frequent heart attacks, and over the years she had suffered from pernicious anaemia and cancer. She deserved a retirement, even if I did not feel quite ready for total inactivity, and so I retired on 30 November 1994, just seven weeks after my sixty-fifth birthday.

Other Spirits

As with most parish priests, I had to deal, from time to time, with strange happenings – the sort usually classified as 'supernatural' or 'spooky'. There were numerous instances of young people dabbling in levitation and Ouija boards, which produced personality problems and disturbing experiences, but there were three main such experiences in Wythenshawe. One concerned a

---

[48] Studying, writing and administration in the morning, visiting around the parish in the afternoon, and meetings almost every evening (with one whole day off on the same day each week – inviolable, except for diocesan meetings or emergencies).

housewife who felt her house was haunted, that there was 'somebody behind me in the room', that she was 'being watched' and subjected to hens eggs which dropped from a clear sky while she was hanging out her washing in the garden. The house was about seven years old, and she was the fifth or sixth tenant. As she was a Roman Catholic, Louis St John dealt with it, in the time-honoured way, and there was no further trouble. I went through a patch of having eggs smashed on the seat of my motorbike while it was parked near the church, but as that is supposed to be a characteristic of Old Nick's playing the nuisance, I cleaned it off each time and carried on as usual. One evening, however, the bike was stolen from outside the church, and I walked slowly home in the darkness, after a very tiring day, and arrived in a state of something less than hilarious high spirits. Joy met me at the door, and was so cross at such a happening, on top of all the usual pressures, that she suggested we prayed for the miscreant there and then, with our daughter, who had joined us. We were still standing in the hall when the doorbell rang. I opened the door, but there seemed to be no one there. On stepping outside, I saw a figure in the gloom, and closer inspection revealed it to be one of the more lawless of the local youths. He had a sheepish look on his face and confessed he had stolen the bike but had had a sudden attack of conscience, and brought it back. And there it was. Another case was associated with a lady in the congregation who was a medium. She had a widespread ministry in South Lancashire, and I discovered that she ran an evening weekday spiritualist service in a room at the civic centre. With her foreknowledge I attended one of them, in 'civvies' and after protecting myself by prayer, to see for myself what theology was on display. It was a fairly straightforward nonconformist-type service of hymns and prayers, with Jesus at the centre, but with an open counselling session instead of a sermon. This showed her as having an impressive sensitivity to individuals' pleas for help, and apparent ability to be of consolation. There was no showmanship, none of the customary run-through of names until she found one that registered, to convince the client that the medium was in touch with Charlie or Fred or Arthur, deceased. My friend regarded this activity as her calling and ministry, and attended

Holy Communion without fail every week to give her the strength to sustain it. After some cautionary words from me, she said she had a Red Indian Guide, who would appear to her at the bedside when she had read her daily Bible passages, and asked if she should continue with him. Quoting I John 4:1–3, I suggested she asked him directly, 'Do you believe that Jesus Christ is God, come in the flesh?' and see how he reacted. The first time she put the question to him, he frowned, and faded away. On the second evening he appeared more faintly, frowned and disappeared; and after the third evening, when he was hardly visible at all, she never saw him again. 'What did that tell you?' I asked her. She replied, 'All I need to know. Jesus is my Lord'. She continued to receive 'clients', but put Jesus, the Holy Spirit and the authority of the Church firmly at the centre of her guidance for them. When I left the parish I was encouraging her to offer for training as a lay reader, but my successor did not agree with any form of women's liturgical ministry, and she later became a faithful and hardworking church warden.

In Durham there were three main cases of the 'supernatural', two of them being students driven to distraction after dabbling openly in spiritualism, and one a stubborn case of haunting which took place when I was away on holiday. They were dealt with in my absence by the official diocesan appointees for such phenomena.[49] The third case involved a young woman in her twenties who lived in a flat not far from the vicarage. She came to me one day complaining of what would usually be described as poltergeist activity – objects flying across the room, her bed shaking violently, an oppressive feeling of an undefined fear. As I stood in her living room, trying to get the feel of the place, she noticed that I was having difficulty breathing; there certainly was some kind of heavy pressure on my chest.

'That's what I have felt, too,' she said. She had a fascination for Egyptology and had a copy of the gold funerary mask of Tutankhamen on the wall. She felt that whatever was causing the trouble seemed to be centred on that object, and I suggested she should get rid of it, which she did. Actual exorcism is a

---

[49] One of these was the archdeacon of Durham, Michael Perry, who has written extensively and authoritatively about such ministry.

dangerous procedure, and is rarely necessary, so I prayed there for a while before going away. For a few days all seemed to be well, and in the meantime I brushed up on poltergeist activity. It seemed there were two theories – one that they are objective, demonic, spiritual entities, which latch on to congenial human activities, or psychological tensions in a house; and the other that claimed they were an extrapolation of the subjective emotional turmoil of a family member, usually a teenage female. The phenomena recurred (though I never witnessed any airborne objects), and we invited her to stay in the vicarage guest room for a day or two, to give her some sleep (she was working full time, and it would have been disastrous for her to lose her job, not to mention her marbles). Before I drew up a more businesslike plan – candles, holy water, more particularised prayers and so on – I discussed the two theories with her, saying that both were speculative. I knew the family well, and that the father was prey to irrational behaviour and had a difficult relationship with his wife and six children. 'You mean I'm causing it all myself?' she said, whereupon I explained that even if the second hypothesis were the only true one, the phenomena were by no means her fault. I suggested we act on both theories, with prayers which took them into account. When I next visited her, she told me that she had been to the spiritualist church. 'Well they're supposed to be the experts, aren't they?' she replied when I expressed some surprise. 'They told me that yes, there is a bad spirit present,[50] but they have invited four good ones to reason with it.' Marvellous, I thought. Now we have several more invaders to deal with. The atmosphere in the room was still bad, but my second 'deliverance service' was successful, and no further trouble occurred.

★

---

[50] In my experience, spiritualists do not seem to distinguish between poltergeists, individual evil spirits, and the souls of the departed. Any invocation of spirits other than the Holy Spirit is asking for the invasion of further trouble, sometimes very serious trouble. Séances, as well as Ouija boards, tarot cards and the like, are well-known methods of running into such deadly quicksands (see Luke 11.24–26).

> Does the fish soar to find the ocean,
> The eagle plunge to find the air –
> That we ask of the stars in motion
> If they have rumour of thee there?[51]

During my time at St Cuthbert's I had two funerals which involved atheists. While visiting a crop of recently occupied new houses in the parish, I came across a retired Danish psychologist. Curious to know what on earth such an unexpected person was doing in Pity Me, a modest ex-colliery village, he explained to me that on returning to Denmark after many years in the USA he had looked at a map of Europe to see where to take his holidays, and was arrested by the number of Scandinavian-based place names in the north-east of England. He holidayed for three successive years in Northumbria, and then decided to move to Durham to live. His house was stacked with books and dozens of cassettes of music, and we soon discovered a mutual enthusiasm for Bruckner, Mahler and the composers of the Second Viennese School. Our conversation often moved in the direction of theology, but sadly he was soon diagnosed as having terminal cancer, and at his funeral I was able to say one of the prayers in Danish, courtesy of one of the members of Joy's Clergy Wives Group, Elizabeth Forster. The brother of the deceased, over from Greenland, along with his son and daughter from Sweden, expressed some surprise that I been asked by him to take a religious service, as he had always declared himself a complete sceptic in such matters.[52] But when I explained that towards the end he had wanted the Bible read to him and questions on it answered, they seemed to be reassured that I had not taken a high hand after his departure.

The other funeral concerned the son and brother of a recently deceased professor of chemistry, who had come to see me one day. He had died as a fiercely convinced atheist, as had a brother of his who had died the year previously. On that occasion, a relative had led a humanist funeral at the crematorium, but every one present had felt a dissatisfaction with the event, and this time

---

[51] Francis Thompson, from the poem 'The Kingdom of God', second stanza.
[52] Though the daughter, on her several visits to him during his last months, always attended church.

had wanted it done 'by a professional', and would I take a non-believer's service for them?

My reply was that my very 'professionalism' came from a firm conviction of the truth of the Christian faith, and they could scarcely expect me to compromise myself. We eventually worked out that the two of them would take away a copy of the funeral service, and come back to me with an indication of the sections they felt could be 'owned' by the family. In the meantime I drew up such a service according to my own judgement and integrity (the modern funeral service is capable of a very great flexibility). To my surprise, the one they returned with was identical to mine. We had lift-off. The son suggested I could in the homily rebuke his father's atheism, but I replied that it would have been quite wrong to take advantage of his enforced inability to reply; I would, however, declare the Christian doctrines of the nature of life and death, and they agreed to that. I was surprised at the warmth of the family's appreciation on the day. Another lesson for me in the truth that the Holy Spirit doesn't need telling what to do, but does what is right in us and through us.

One of the last items of new responsibility in the early 1990s was to be asked to act as deputy to the diocesan director of clergy training. Having had twenty-seven or twenty-eight ordinands on placement sequentially over the sixteen years at St Cuthbert's,[53] I felt quite at home with twelve or fifteen all at once. The question of accepting extra-parochial responsibility had been a problem with me over the years. I still wonder sometimes whether I was right in 1984 and the two occasions following,[54] to refuse nomination for election as chairman of the house of clergy in the diocesan synod. I did agree to serve, at his request, on the Bishops' Council for a term (three years), but resisted repeated suggestions from fellow clergy to stand for election to the General Synod. It struck me several years later that some of those refusals might have been seen as a betrayal of my

---

[53] I had one previous placement, a former Mormon bishop who had become an Anglican and offered for ordination, who was placed with me when I was in Wythenshawe by Canon Michael Hennell of Manchester Cathedral.

[54] One from the floor of the synod, and the others at four-year intervals, by request from the diocesan staff to stand, as there had been no nomination before the meeting. I agreed, provided that no one was proposed from the meeting itself, which they were.

colleagues' wishes and of their confidence. But I could honestly say that I had no ambitions, let alone a 'career structure plan'.[55]

Durham had been a wonderful place to live. The historic spirituality and sheer inspiration of Aidan, Cuthbert and Bede seemed to be a living heritage, and I have an enduring recollection of the people I met there. My choice (between Liverpool and Durham) of the venue of my ministerial selection conference in 1958 (St John's College, Durham) proved to be prophetic of my going in 1973 to work in the diocese, and I shall always cherish the memories.

---

[55] I met very few clergy who had. One I knew, however, had early declared to a church warden that he was going to become a diocesan bishop; and so he did, and a very good one, too.

5

Post-retirement Postlude

The best is yet to come.[1]

Joy and I had spent a brief and pleasant holiday in Nantwich, Cheshire on our post-Christmas break in 1988, at the apropos-of-nothing recommendation of a parishioner who happened to have been stationed near there in the RAF during the war. [2] When we came to think of retiring six years later we looked at houses in Lanchester (Durham), Gateshead and Maryport (Cumbria) dock developments and Harlech, but nothing seemed to 'click'. I noticed in the *Church Times* an advertisement from the rector of 'a church in a large market town' for a recently retired priest to serve as a house-for-duty curate. I recognised the telephone code (01270) as Crewe, and a reference to *Crockford's Clerical Directory* revealed the phone number as that of the Rector of Nantwich. So I applied for the job, went for interview, but didn't get it, because the other applicant was happier to fill the need for help with the ten old people's homes in the parish, whereas I felt my gifts to be more in the realm of young people's work. We decided to go there, however, and found a highly suitable house (bought by the Pensions Board) – off the main road but within easy walking of the church, the railway station, the health centre, dentists, the osteopath, the corner shop (actually a supermarket), theatre, library, restaurants, banks, building societies and the River Weaver: it seemed perfect. Alas, less than eight months later Joy

---

[1] Michael Ramsey.
[2] Nobody had ever before mentioned Nantwich to us at all, and my only knowledge of the town, as a Cheshire man, apart from its being a rather attractive black-and-white building sort of place, was of passing through it on several journeys to and from the Market Drayton Sanatorium in 1954 and 1955.

was dead. We had had a wonderful pilgrimage to Israel in May 1995, and having been halfway to heaven at the holy sites, with a particularly blessed visit to the Garden Tomb in Jerusalem, she seemed thereafter to be looking for the other half of the journey. Her death, coming unexpectedly after a totally successful hip operation in July 1995, was beautiful – touched with, and graded by, the hand of God. She had been a constant source of patient support of my ministry, through the ravages of diabetes and all the other ailments, and despite my many failings and weaknesses.

During the years 1995 to 1997 I was much used by the rector in services, study groups, helping (after all) with the services in old people's homes, and with confirmation classes. I entered into a full and enjoyable life with the church choir, which was run by a first-class musician and had over forty members, half of whom were children. But I began to miss the responsibility and full immersion in parish life. The congregation at Nantwich had seven or eight retired priests, half of whom had been forced by ill health, mental or physical, to retire, some before sixty-five. And there I was, climbing mountains, playing five-a-side football with the youth group and feeling unsettled at having given up my vocation after less than thirty-four years. My participation in the youth work of a parish mission held in Nantwich in the autumn of 1996 moved the missioner, the archdeacon of Stoke-on-Trent, after the final rally in the civic hall, to suggest to me that I was too young to retire and would I like another job?

In those words he echoed what Bishop Jack Spong of Newark, New Jersey had said when I met him in Durham Cathedral in December 1994; but I did not think I would have fitted in well with his theology! On this occasion, however, I replied strongly in the affirmative, and thus began, in May 1997, a 'second' career. Times had changed even in the short while I had been out of office: I had to get references to certify that I was fit to be in contact with children, and I was officially interviewed, among four other candidates, by the four church wardens of Sandon and Salt,[3] near Stafford.[4] They were an interesting pairing of parishes:

---

[3] The Archdeacon's original intention was to send me to Holy Angels, Hoar Cross, near Burton on Trent – a beautiful G F Bodley Gothic Revival building, listed

Sandon was the church of the estate of the Earl of Harrowby, and stood in the grounds of Sandon Hall. The earls had a strong tradition of evangelicalism, and, like so many estate churches, adhered firmly to the (1662) *Book of Common Prayer*. Salt, at the other extreme, was in the patronage of Keble College, Oxford, and was strongly of the Catholic tradition. There were two other churches in the benefice, one sharing Sandon's ethos, and the other a daughter church of Salt. After a year or two, Lord Harrowby, the patron, and the Bishop of Stafford both asked me how I was getting on, riding two horses in such a way. As I explained, I had never regarded 'churchmanship' as totally defining. Rather I chose to adhere to what was positive in Catholic tradition (loyalty to historical continuity, reverence for the sacramental principle and for traditional order and discipline), evangelical (accepting the Bible as the revealed word of God, the importance of sound preaching, and the reality of the conversion experience), and liberal (a willingness to learn from other religious traditions, and from all the spheres of human insight – science, art, literature, and so on); and to the charismatic theology of the power of the Holy Spirit (God working at the coal face of human existence). In this, I was humbled but thrilled when the last student of the twenty-eight or so I had had on placement in Durham from theological courses[5] told me how he had filled in his final report to the director of one of the Midlands training schemes. To the question of the churchmanship of his last placement, he answered, totally unprompted by me, in the above terms. We had not discussed the subject as such, but he had discerned my position in action. I have to admit, however, that to be at Salt, a church with a completely 'Catholic' tradition of

---

Grade 1, dating from 1876, built as a memorial by the Meynell family. But it had only a tiny parish and therefore was difficult for the diocese to staff easily. The bishop of Stafford apparently thought I was capable of taking on a larger responsibility than that.

[4] Oddly enough I had earlier met the outgoing vicar in 1995, because he had retired to Crewe.

[5] Only two of whom were women. Sue Hope, at Cranmer Hall via the York parish of St Michael-le-Belfry, who is (in 2006) Canon Missioner in the diocese of Sheffield; and Claire Lofgren, from the Church Divinity School of the Pacific (USA), via Peter Baelz, whose father was part of the team which produced the first atom bomb. She is currently chaplain to a convent in New York State.

The 12th century parish church of All Saints, Sandon (Harrowby Estate)

*The 11th century parish church of All Saints, Standon, North Staffordshire.
Photograph by Rosemary Walken*

worship – incense and all – was a delight. There were two first-class Sunday school teachers (they were so good that none of the children wanted to leave after confirmation), with about nine children aged nine to fourteen, and they formed the nucleus of a team of altar servers, as well as a confirmation class. During my time of almost three years there – holding the fort until the processes of the legal formation of a team ministry based in Weston, the next village, had been completed – I had been commuting back to Nantwich on a Sunday afternoon to work with the youth fellowship. This was a group of young lads who wouldn't attend the Bible study in the church hall after Evensong (in which I continued my membership of the bass line of the choir) unless it began with a half-hour session of five-a-side soccer. I was happy to lead the latter and leave the study part to the curate and his wife and an earnest and hard-working member of the choir (a female tenor). When I finally severed my connection with South Cheshire, I attached myself to the local authority youth club[1] in Sandon village hall, and joined in all their activities until I left. Salt and Sandon were very pleasant parishes to serve in, and there are some outstanding servants of God there. William Sargent had been a farmer on the Sandon Estate for nearly all his working life, and a notable figure in farming circles. He was church warden there for fifty years, retiring at the age of eighty-five. Salt, too, was blessed with two dedicated church wardens, and a consistent benefactor (who died while I was there, sadly). It is a joyful realisation that wherever a priest finds him- or herself working, there are saintly people, unknown and unsung beyond their own area, faithfully serving God, day by day.

The second appointment that the bishop of Stafford commended to me was to move to the north-west of Stafford, to the Eccleshall deanery. To serve the twenty churches in that deanery, there were, after Easter 2000, to be only two and a half clergy because of

---

[1] It was interesting to note that with the young people there, despite the fact that I played in 'uniform', the five-a-sides were far more clashingly physical than those in Nantwich, where I was not known by the youngsters to be a priest. Young people respect in some way a priest's spiritual authority, but are reluctant to allow him or her any competence in their own field, and take a dim view of any ability to beat them on their own ground.

the (unplanned) simultaneous retirement of all the others. I was asked to be 'deanery pastoral assistant', originally with a deanery commitment to helping wherever necessity decreed, living in the vicarage of Croxton parish. As it turned out, the church wardens of each of the parishes were so diligent that they had 'staffed' their services for the whole of their interregna with retired priests from the Stafford deanery, and so I became simply the priest in charge of Croxton and Broughton, and after some months, on the departure of the 'half priest', of Standon and Cotes Heath as well. One happy coincidence was that Broughton parish was just the other side of Bishop's Wood from the TB sanatorium (closed in the late 1960s) where I had been converted forty-six years before. I found the actual spot of my illumination on the housing estate which had been built on the site in the 1970s, and discovered that the house there belonged to a leader of the parish (Ashley)[2] youth club, who promptly signed me up as an associate leader. The liveliest of the four churches was All Saints, Standon, an eleventh-century church with a church warden, Geoff Clark, whose father and grandfather before him had held the same office for as long as anyone could remember. It had a group of young women who had come to firm faith, under a previous incumbent, through the Alpha Course, and they had an enthusiastic ministry to children and young people in the parish, having been given a free hand with services for them. It was to be expected that they would be extremely wary of an old 'school of 1958' priest, who suggested that they brought their charges into a full-scale Eucharistic service with the main congregation on Easter morning.

'It would be far too long for the children,' they argued, 'beyond their attention span,' (totally boring, by implication). However, I had extensive experience with children's Eucharists, and knew that with strong planning and disciplined presentation, such a service could be made to last not longer than forty-five minutes. We put together an agreed form in which they would conduct the synaxis (the ministry of the word, including an instructional address), and I would lead the second half, the ministry of the sacrament – without a sermon from me! That

---

[2] Of whom the patrons were the Meynell Trust. Several 'full circles' were being formed at the time! (cf.p.134, note)

Easter morning was a most joyful affair: the service ran as planned (except that the presentation or exposition part of it ran five minutes over, but no one was dismayed by that). We had present between seventy and eighty people, right across the age range – more (other than at funerals and weddings), said Geoff Clark afterwards, than he could remember ever seeing in the church before. It was wonderful to know that, even though the Holy Spirit of God never changes, it was still possible for Him to work through old and battered flesh.

The bishop had wanted me to commit myself there initially for two or two and half years, but I said I thought eighteen months might prove to be enough, which turned out to be correct. With the best will in the world, I was eventually finding the travelling between four churches tiring, especially with the pastoral pressure of the foot-and-mouth disease outbreak, and by the time that period had elapsed my health was beginning to suffer.[3] That area of North Staffordshire is known as 'the Woodland Quarter', and it had far more than its fair share of notable residents. One man, who seemed to have been there since the 1930s, was a trained carpenter working with the RAF in Stafford, and in the church. He had been a stalwart of the parish church nearly all his life, nominally the verger, but fulfilling all manner of roles, and because of his collection of memorabilia of the parish could quote all the names of incumbents and curates, from its foundation in 1857. He sang in the church choirs at Croxton and Broughton as a tenor almost to the end at the age of ninety-two. An organist was an ex-guardsman, ex-policeman, ex-schoolteacher, who was the inspiration behind getting a memorial to A E Housman placed in Westminster Abbey. There was an old Etonian, who had been a professional film producer before applying his talents to making a video record of the history of the Woodland Quarter and of local characters. Aiding and abetting him in the interviews for the videos was a most unexpected man, John Myatt,[4] who, having

---

[3] As it happened, an appointment was made to the four-parish benefice less than three months after my final retirement to Shrewsbury.

[4] He was a distant relative of mine. My mother's father was also called John Myatt and was born in the same place, Barlaston in Staffordshire.

trained as a chorister in Worcester Cathedral Choir School, became a professional pop musician (he had two of his songs in the Top Ten in the 1970s), and was choirmaster at Croxton Church.[5] His main claim to fame and infamy, however, is that, as an art teacher, he was sent to prison in 1999 for painting imitations of the works of old masters and selling them as originals. He was thoroughly encouraged and exploited in this by a third party, however, and having served only a nominal sentence, he has since set up an agency named 'Genuine Fakes', producing almost indistinguishable reproductions of famous paintings as commissions, and staging exhibitions from time to time in the Midlands and in London.

One enjoyable engagement of the last weeks before my final 'retirement' was to address the clergy of the Stafford Episcopal area who were approaching sixty-five, on the range of possibilities of continuing employment. I had been preparing clergy for the unexpected traumas of retirement for my last ten years in Durham diocese and although, as with training for bereavement counselling, all the preparation in the world does not prepare one fully for when it happens to oneself, I was convinced that a certain pre-wisdom was valuable and would justify itself eventually. The diocese of Lichfield had a remarkably flexible and systematic way of dealing with clergy who wished to continue their ministry after pensionable age. These ranged from allowing them to work until they were seventy; staying on in their parish on a 'house for duty' basis; taking up a new appointment of virtually full-time commitment on half pay; a sliding scale of one third or one quarter stipend in a parish hard to fill; or on a term of contract to see a parish, or group of parishes, through to pastoral reorganisation. It seemed to me to be a fully realistic way of using the gifts and energies of retired clergy in a positive and responsible manner. The policy did not seem to harm the development of lay ministry and local ordained ministry at all. I declined an earnest and repeated invitation to deliver a similar message to a gathering of

---

[5] I joined the choir there and had a wonderful time. This choir (like that of Nantwich church) enjoyed 'cathedral choir locum' status, and appeared at Liverpool, Chester, Worcester and other cathedrals.

priests in the Lichfield area, on the grounds that it was specifically concerned with house-for-duty priests. I had no experience of such appointments, and had grave misgivings about them. An illustration of this was when I applied, just before I retired finally from Eccleshall deanery, for details of a house-for-duty appointment not very far away, and was dismayed to find that the expectations were pretty much identical to those for a new incumbent. The specification, for two churches, was for visiting throughout the parish, going into the Church school twice a week, house communions (especially in the old people's homes), vigorous cultivation of youth work and so on. The expectation of six days a week availability, especially for funerals and weddings, seems almost universal and inevitable in that kind of contract. It was the customary 'Archangel Gabriel' expectation, so familiar to bishops and patrons for full-time appointments, but with vastly less possibility of realisation. I did not apply formally. Such agreements need to be strictly delineated and understood beforehand if they are to be satisfactory.

All these post-retirement years were marked, as before, by wonderful happenings and so-called 'happy coincidences'. They were years of 'all things working together for good for those who love the Lord', and of vivid answers to the prayer 'Go before us O Lord, in these and all our doings', despite the occasional shortcomings on my part. I retired to a new house in Shrewsbury, but in my final retirement house in South Shropshire I have been appointed as assistant priest to the female vicar of my present parish. I prayed when I retired that I would be of assistance to whatever parish priest I was parishioner, especially if a woman priest, because they have less support from tradition in their ministry. She has four parishes, eventually to be extended to seven.

It is customary, and therefore expected, that an old priest, faced with such bewildering changes in society and in the Church as there have been in the last ten or so years, should have the feeling of having got off the train while those still on board are enjoying the journey to the next station. It is also expected that he should feel bereft (and it is a real bereavement, no matter what the cynics may say) and experience concern and some genuine responsibility for the work of God's

Kingdom, and be critical of the second and third generations of clergy since his own for 'not being of the same standard'. It is true, I think, that dedication to the concepts of excellence, of best practice, and strict self-discipline in clergy formation have slipped, under strong condemnation from postmodernist charges of 'elitism', as belonging to a bygone age. It also derives in part, I feel, from the influence of the introduction of women to the ministry, bringing with them more heart and emotion to the job than the old head-ruled and objective attitude which so characterises the other gender, and from the influence of 'emancipated wives' to the ordained ministry – a more 'family-centred' mode of ministering than the previous 'monastic' style. But the briefest of encounters with a selection of parish priests have been enough for me to carry conviction of just as devout a commitment to the work of God, and mostly in far more testing circumstances than those of thirty or forty years ago. They go about their business in housing estates in Walsall, Wakefield and Manchester, in inner city parishes and sprawling suburbs, and in multi-church country benefices, with dedication and with a buoyant sense of faith and hope and humour. (Indeed, in some areas to try to sustain a ministry without a sense of the ridiculous is to court disaster). They are not as well-supported by 'tradition' or, alas, in pastoral care as we were, except in certain dioceses. They are assailed much more frequently than we were by reorganisation, reassessments, new initiatives,[6] strictures on their financial administration and pastoral flexibility (because of the antics of a few unscrupulous clergy of my generation) and by assessment of their 'efficiency' at regular intervals, which may be helpful 'counselling sessions' to some but to others may inculcate reinforcement of the all-too-frequent reminders of inadequacy. So many changes, each following hard on the heels of the last, all requiring more paperwork, and with so many attacks on well-tested

---

[6] A retired bishop friend gives vent to his sadness in reporting that the bishop of his diocese cares very little for matters pastoral, preferring constant administrative tinkering; and an archdeacon (of a different diocese), on being asked how things were going, sighed, and said he was 'assailed by a surfeit of initiatives'. It is the same elsewhere: Benedict XVI, contemplating the Vatican curia, has said, 'What the Church needs is holiness, not management... It needs saints, not functionaries.' *The Ratzinger Report* (Ignatius Press: St Francisco, 1985) pp.63 and 67.

administration and theology, all raise the question of where, if anywhere, our faith and ministry finds its bedrock. Even those of strongest faith and commitment can suffer insecurity when they can't feel firm ground beneath their feet.

It is noticeable, however, that even in the most recent publications, the guidelines for the practical formation of deacons and priests still follow recognisable patterns and presuppositions, despite the seismic changes of the last forty years. Anyone who reads Charles Forder's *The Parish Priest at Work*[7] will recognise the basic methods and priorities set out in current handbooks. The analysis of the job as outlined in Michael Ramsey's *The Christian Priest Today*[8] still offers great depth and guidance to those preparing for ministry in the twenty-first century. Another helpful book, among many, first published in 1988 and given added interest by developments in this century, is *Ministers of Your Joy*[9], a series of ordination retreat addresses by Joseph Ratzinger. The book is notable for its profound exposition of passages of scripture relevant to the ministry. A book on preaching which I found to be foundational, though it is perhaps less practically ideal, was W A Sangster's *The Art of the Sermon*. I started off on my exploration of vocation by being prepared for the Methodist ministry,[10] and I have attempted always to recognise the importance of being soundly well-prepared, well-researched, 'prayed in', simply expressed and related to life, in all preaching. Whatever our chosen model, the decay of Bible-based preaching nowadays is a sad loss to the people of God. The Bible, by its nature and purpose, is inexhaustible, and can never be made redundant in preaching. The incorporation of lay people in the ministry, a great blessing when it is done thoroughly, is all too often a conscription of bewildered and half-unwilling folks who are given no training at all, but left to make what they can of what they are asked to do.[11] No wonder so many

---

[7] Society for the Propagation of Christian Knowledge, 1959 and many reprints.
[8] Society for the Propagation of Christian Knowledge, 1972, 1985, 1987, 1992, etc.
[9] Republished in 2005, on the author's elevation to highest office.
[10] I took my first public (as distinct from sanatorium chapel) service at the Methodist chapel at Carrington, South Lancashire. It closed not long afterwards.
[11] It is a policy which gives the impression that training, formation and learning are not necessary, because everyone's idea and opinions are as valid as anyone else's, and the most distressing messages are therefore sometimes heard in sermons. It is hard not to be of the opinion, despite all attempts to think modern and accept

priests and readers are demoralised about their vocation. The modern development of 'shared ministry', the appointment of certain of the laity in each parish to share the ministry of the incumbent,[12] too often, in its amorphous expectations, leads to bewilderment. It even gives rise to questions why the clergy need such amplified support, when their commitment to the job is apparently, sometimes, less than it was in a previous dispensation. Like the GP, who now works four and a half days a week instead of the old six days a week,[13] modern clergy seem to be nowhere near as available as they used to be, and family and friends seem to take first priority over pastoral care of the benefice. The laity see themselves as working full time and yet are still expected to perform the duties of one who is paid full time to do them. However, it is a fact of the changing times, and we must attempt to cope creatively with it. All denominations, at least in Europe, seem to be experiencing difficulties in sustaining a traditional full-time ministry, with a thorough-going educational and spiritual formation. This is largely, though not entirely, due to financial strictures. The Church of England, for instance, is not short, most years, of candidates for ordination, but of money to pay them and to prepare for their pensions. We may have to adopt the pattern of the Pentecostal churches and train and employ as a norm non-stipendiary ministers who have full-time employment in other work. Or we might, at any rate in new ('church planting') projects adopt the medieval Jewish principle of deciding where to appoint full-time rabbis; that is, wherever there are ten families to form a synagogue. This, on the basis of tithing, would ensure that there would be sufficient income to pay one stipend.[14]

---

change, that some of the laity are not being schooled in orthodoxy, or being prepared adequately for the new responsibilities being laid upon them.

[12] This has always been with us, but in a structured, step-by-step and recognisable ordering of training and licensing.

[13] According to a GP writing in *The Times* in April 2006.

[14] The main problem in the Church of England is that of the maintenance of buildings. The diocese of Hereford, for instance, has over 450 churches, 95% of which are listed Grade I or II*.Some congregations are too small to afford the maintenance of such treasures. In some places, the parish church has been closed, but taken over by the villagers as a corporate asset. This has produced community support for the repairs of the building, and a quadrupled attendance at services, the diocese providing an authorised ministry.

Whatever method we adopt, in a country rapidly becoming more multi-cultural, a calling is still a calling, and ministry in the Church of God is still essential, challenging, exciting and rewarding. The picture regarding expansion and growth is different in other parts of the world from that of Europe. China, booming economically, is also reported to be producing hundreds of new Christians daily.

The following figures are very heartening:

- 70% of Church growth since its inception took place in the twentieth century;
- 70% of this growth was after the Second World War;
- 70% of this post-war growth took place in the last five years of the century.

★

Any person who [devotes himself] to the cause of the Apostolic Church [...] is sure that sooner or later, his will be the winning side, and that the victory will be complete, universal, eternal.[15]

---

[15] John Keble, Assize Sermon, 14 July 1833.

Lightning Source UK Ltd.
Milton Keynes UK
UKHW041824071118
331952UK00001B/12/P

9 781844 019984